כֹּה עָשׂוּ חֲכָמֵינוּ

❦❦❦❦❦❦❦❦❦❦❦❦

Our Sages
showed the way

כֹּה עָשׂוּ חֲכָמֵינוּ

❁❁❁❁❁❁❁❁❁❁❁❁❁❁❁❁❁❁❁❁❁❁

Translated from the Hebrew by
Esther Falk
Illustrated by
Naama Nothman

VOLUME ONE

YOCHEVED SEGAL

OUR SAGES SHOWED THE WAY

*Stories for young readers and listeners
from the Talmud, Midrash,
and the literature of the Sages*

FELDHEIM PUBLISHERS

Jerusalem • New York

Preface to the English edition

To our readers, young ones and grownups alike:
Shalom!

With thanks to God in our heart, we are glad that this book is at last in your hands. Ever since it first appeared in Hebrew here in the Land of Israel, seventeen years ago, there has been a pressing request to have it translated into English. Parents in other lands have wanted it for their children, teachers for their pupils, Israeli children for their relatives and friends in English-speaking countries.

But as our Sages (blessed be their memory) said, "Everything depends on its own *mazal* (luck), even a Torah-scroll in the Holy Ark" (*Zohar, naso* 134). And so it was not until now that the translation could actually appear.

You might ask, "But why do we need this book? Don't we have enough books to read? There are hundreds, perhaps thousands, of children's books — and good ones, too!"

Of course, that is quite true. But then, you should know that this is not an ordinary children's book, even if it looks like one and was written especially for young readers. "What does that mean?" you wonder. Please let me explain:

Our book contains forty-three *aggadoth*, stories told us by our Sages of blessed memory. Many of them were written in the Talmud (*Bavli* and *Yerushalmi*).

5 🌾

That means they are part of the *Torah she-be'al peh*, that part of the Torah which was handed down by word of mouth from Rabbi to disciple (pupil) and was written down only much later. Other *aggadoth* were gathered by some of our Sages in such important books as *Midrash Rabbah, Yalkut Shimoni* and *Midrash Tanchuma.*

So you see, these stories are not new. Your own father and mother may have read them when they were young.

Now our Sages, of blessed memory, never meant to tell us some nice and interesting stories just to entertain us and make us happy. Every story, even every phrase and almost every word were meant to teach us Torah; to explain something difficult; to make us better, wiser people; to show us how our forefathers and our great leaders and teachers fulfilled the *mitzvoth,* the commandments of God.

For example, they wanted to teach us how to honor our father and mother; how to love our fellowmen; how to love God and pray to Him; and to be gentle and helpful to His creatures; how to trust Him and not to despair even in danger; how to learn Torah with awe and love, and to work honestly; and so on.

So if you are a parent or a teacher who tells the *aggadoth* of our Sages, you are actually teaching Torah; and if you are a young person reading this book or listening to the stories, you are learning Torah. And that is quite a different thing from merely reading a children's book, isn't it?

"But," you may ask now, "will the children like it?

Perhaps there are some children who do not like to listen and to learn. And will they understand? Most *aggadoth* have deep meanings, even mysterious ones, which only great scholars can understand. None is so simple as it might seem at first. Perhaps they might be too difficult for children altogether? Will they have any influence then, as our Sages intended they should? As we all know, children are much more impressed by actions than by words."

Believe me, I myself was quite troubled by such questions when I was asked by the Israeli Ministry of Education, many years ago, to write *aggadoth* in such a manner that even children in the kindergarten would be able to understand them. In fact, I was almost afraid to try. But then I knew this was important work. The thoughts of our Sages, blessed be their memory, *had* to reach our children. And I knew in my heart that it could be done, because our Torah is alive forever. It is fitting forever and for all ages.

So I began the work with awe and love. I began to learn and to write, using the explanations of our great Sages and scholars such as Rashi, consulting our learned instructors (*talmidey chachamim*), trying not to change any important detail in the *aggadoth*, but only to write them in simple and understandable language.

Now, as I mentioned, our Sages did not just tell a story nor did they use any unnecessary words. They wrote in a very short and concentrated way. Therefore, they did not tell us, for example, exactly how Bar-Kamtza looked and felt when he was chased away so rudely from the party (see the story on page 71) or what the lost jewels of the Roman queen were (see the story on page 95). Such details they left for us to imagine — and so I did. Sometimes I also found it necessary to add some explanation into the story, if it was too difficult to understand otherwise. Therefore, it became impossible that there should be no differences whatever between the *aggadoth* in this book and their originals in the sources.

Now, if you are a grownup or a big boy or girl, and you want to know just how a certain *aggadah* was told by our Sages, you might be interested to look up its source. You will find the source listed at the end of each story. Sometimes there are even several sources that you might look up. I'm sure you will learn alot if you do! (Let me include here a plea to our very young readers: Please remember that this is no ordinary book, and try to keep it clean and whole, as befitting a book with stories from our Sages of blessed memory!)

"All right," you might say now, "that's how you dealt with the problem. But what about the children in the Land of Israel? Did they understand? Did they love the stories? And did they grow to be better persons, better members of the Jewish people?"

Well, as for the children, till now several tens of thousands of them (may they multiply) have read the book in Hebrew, and many more have heard the stories told them by their parents or their teachers, or from the radio, which has broadcast many of them. And not only once did they read or listen, but many times, as they and their parents keep telling us, until they knew them almost by heart. So what do you think: Did they understand them, and did they love them?

If the *aggadoth* have helped somebody to be better, I really don't know for sure. That takes perhaps more than mere admiration and respect for our great Sages, more than merely reading and even knowing how one *should* be and act. But — shouldn't you at least give it a try?

And may God help you to succeed and send you His blessings!

Yocheved Segal

Jerusalem
Tammuz 5739 (June 1979)

❦ contents

Trust in God

Trust in God

In a faraway city there lived a very rich man, who had a spacious home with expensive furnishings and a lovely garden lush with trees and many flowers. He could afford to buy whatever his heart desired. Yet in spite of his wealth, he was not happy, because he lived all alone in the big house. He had no family — no father and no mother; no wife and no children. The man was very lonely and sad.

He thought to himself, "What good is all my money? Should I buy food for myself? Indeed I have already had my fill of all the delicacies. Shall I buy more clothes? All my closets are full. Shall I acquire possessions? There is no one to enjoy them. When I die, who will have all my wealth? If only I were able to make someone happy with it!" And so the man was always worried and miserable. His neighbors, who saw that he was unhappy, heard his complaints and said to him, "We have good advice for you: distribute your money among the poor. You will make them happy with your

17 🌹

help, and at the same time you will do a good deed just as God commanded in the Torah."

The rich man listened to their advice and decided to follow their suggestion. "Yes, I shall do so! But I will not give my money just to any beggar collecting alms on the street. I will give it only to a man like myself, who has no one in the whole wide world to help him. He will certainly be very happy with the money that I give him."

The man took a large purse filled with coins of silver and looked among the poor for a man who lived alone and was helpless, but such a man was not to be found. One man was helped by his children, a second man by his relatives, a third by his neighbors, and a fourth man by good people who fulfilled the commandment of giving charity to the poor. The man searched and searched but could not find a person who was all alone in the world and really had no one to help him.

One day while the man was taking a walk in the countryside, he saw a poor, wretched stranger sitting on a big pile of stones. The man was very thin, his clothes were torn and shabby, but he appeared to be happy and gay.

"Why are you sitting here?" asked the rich man.

"Because I have no other place. I own no house and no room, and I don't have a garden in which to sit down and relax," answered the stranger.

"Why is your face so thin?" asked the rich man.

"Because I have not had anything to eat for a long time," was the reply.

The rich man wanted to make certain that the stranger was penniless and destitute, so he asked, "Why are your clothes so shabby?"

"Because they are old and I have no other clothes," the stranger replied.

The rich man asked, "Don't you have any relatives or neighbors or friends to help you?"

"I have no one," said the poor man.

"At long last, I have found the man I have been looking for," thought the rich man. "He has no one to help him. Let me give him my money!"

The rich man took his purse and gave it to the stranger. The poor man stared at it in amazement and exclaimed, "Why are you giving me so much money? There are certainly other poor people in the city to whom you can give charity. Why are you giving it all to me?"

"Because," said the rich man, "I have decided to give the money only to a man who has no one else in the whole wide world to help him and you are such a man."

Upon hearing this, the poor man returned the purse to his benefactor and exclaimed: "God forbid! I didn't say that! There may be no man in the world to help me, but God will have pity on me

19 🌸

and will help me in the end. I am sure of that. Please take your money back, for you gave it to me by mistake!"

The rich man looked up in disappointment. "If that is the case, there is no person to whom I can give my wealth!" he thought. So he dug a hole in the earth, hid his purse in it, and returned home. And God, Who is aware of everything, saw what the rich man had done. He was not pleased with the deed, and so he caused the rich man to lose all his wealth and become poor. At first he was forced to sell his beautiful garden and his expensive furniture. Next he had to sell his big house and everything in it, until he had nothing left.

Then he remembered the purse that he had hidden in the ground and he thought to himself: "I will go and I will take it for myself. How lucky I am that I still have something left!" So he went to the hole in the ground in which he had hidden his purse, and while he was searching, two policemen passed by and they saw him digging.

"What are you looking for?" they asked him.

"I am looking for my money which I hid here," the man said.

"*Your* money, you say!" exclaimed one of the policemen. "You must have stolen it, I am sure. Otherwise you would not have had to hide it. Come with us to the ruler of the town and he will decide how to punish you!" So the policemen took the man and brought him before the ruler. And the man wept and said to him, "Please believe me, your honor. This is truly my money and I did not steal it. I hid it only because I couldn't find anyone who deserved it," he pleaded.

The ruler looked hard and, recognizing his old benefactor, said kindly, "Don't you recognize me? I am that same poor man who did not want to accept your money. Looking at me, you see that God can help everyone — even the poor man who has nothing. God had pity on me and helped me and now I have become the ruler of the city. Don't you cry either!" added the kind ruler. "I know that you are not a thief and that the purse is yours. You may take it." And he added, "Why should you always be lonely and sad? I invite you to live in my beautiful home and to eat with me at my table!"

The man remained at the home of the ruler and lived in contentment. From this kind man he learned to trust in God and await His help.

Source: Rabbi Nissim Gaon, *Sefer haMa'asiyoth*

Whatever God does,
He does for the best

Rabbi Akiba once went on a long journey, and he took with him a donkey, a rooster, and a candle. He took along the donkey so that he could ride it when he was tired and so that it would carry burdens which were too heavy for him.

Why did he take the rooster? The rooster, he thought, would wake him at dawn with the familiar call, "Cock-a-doodle-doo."

Why did he take the candle? So that he could light it at night and study Torah by the light of the burning flame.

Very early one morning Rabbi Akiba arose and said his prayers. Then he went on his way.

He traveled a long way until he came to a city. When night came and darkness fell, he decided to stop at an inn for the night. But there was no inn to be found in the entire city!

Rabbi Akiba asked the people of the town to let him stay for the night, but the people said, "We have no room for you! Go on!"

Rabbi Akiba stood outside in the dark and

cold, but no one invited him in. And yet in spite of that he said, "Whatever God does, He does for the best."

He did not want to remain in a city so unfriendly to a stranger, so he went out into the field. There he put his little saddle under a tree, lit the candle, fed the donkey and the rooster, and then he sat down to study the Torah. He forgot that he was all alone in the field in the dark of night.

Suddenly Rabbi Akiba heard a terrible roar, and he saw a fierce lion jump from the thick of the forest and tear the donkey. He was still standing frightened and bewildered when a cat came and devoured the rooster; and before he had a chance to save the rooster from the cat, a gust of wind blew and put out the candle, and he remained in complete darkness.

He had nothing left. The donkey was gone. The rooster was dead, and the candle was out. And yet even then Rabbi Akiba said, "Whatever God does He does for the best."

Suddenly he heard an alarming uproar from the city in which he had wanted to stay overnight. There were cries for help and loud shouting. What terrible thing had happened?

That very night enemies had attacked the city and taken all the people prisoner. They had even passed through the field where Rabbi Akiba had stayed for the night, but in the dark they could not see him, and so he was saved from danger and his life was spared.

Rabbi Akiba realized what had happened and he said, "Now everyone can see that whatever God does He does for the best. If the lion had not devoured the donkey, it would have brayed; if the cat hadn't eaten the the rooster he would have crowed; and if the wind hadn't put out the candle it would have lit up the darkness. Then the soldiers would have found me and put me in prison, too."

Rabbi Akiba thanked God for saving him and he went on his way in peace.

Source: Talmud Bavli, Berachoth 60b

Nachum Ish Gam-zu

any years ago there lived a wise and good man in Israel and his name was Nachum Ish Gam-zu. Why was he called Gam-zu? Because whenever anything happened he always said, "*Gam zu le-tova* — this too is for the best. Whatever God does, He does for the best."

It happened once that the Jewish people who lived in the Land of Israel said, "We shall send a gift to the king of the Romans, so that he will not make war on us!"

And so they did. They took a box full of precious stones and pearls, a present for the Roman king. But who would carry the box to the king? Who would guard the precious stones on the long journey from the Land of Israel to Rome? The road was dangerous. There might be a storm at sea, or robbers might steal the box.

Where could they find an honest and trustworthy man to carry the exquisite gems to the king?

Then they thought of Nachum Ish Gam-zu. "We will send our faithful Rabbi!" they said.

Nachum agreed to take the box to the king because he wanted to help his people. And so he started out on the distant and dangerous journey without fear. "This, too, is for the best," he repeated to himself.

Nachum Ish Gam-zu traveled on a ship for many days, and then he walked on foot all day until he reached an inn to rest during the night.

Tired, Nachum said his prayers and lay down to sleep. He put the box with the valuable gift down beside him.

The innkeeper saw the strange box. He was very curious to find out what was in it. So when Nachum Ish Gam-zu fell asleep, the innkeeper came over quietly and opened the box. Oh, how the precious stones sparkled! The innkeeper stood long and looked hard at the treasure. He wanted it very much! If only he could have it, he thought. At last, he did something very wicked — he took out the pearls and the precious stones, and he put dirt and pebbles in the box instead. Then he carefully closed the box and went to sleep.

Nachum Ish Gam-zu woke up early the next morning. He said his morning prayers, took the box and went to the palace of the king.

When he came before the king, Nachum said to

him, "Greetings, your majesty! I have brought you a beautiful gift from the Jewish people of the Land of Israel."

The king saw the pretty box, and he, too, was very curious about its contents. With great anticipation, he opened it, and what do you think he found? Dirt! Dirt and a few small stones.

The king's face flushed with anger. "What is this?" he called out. "Do you call this a beautiful gift? Don't I have enough dirt and stones in my courtyard? I see that the Jews are making fun of me! I will punish them, and the man who brought the box will be put to death at once!"

But Nachum Ish Gam-zu was not at all afraid. As usual, he said, "This, too, is for the best. Whatever God does, He does for the best!"

God saw that Nachum had trust in Him, and so He sent Elijah the Prophet to save him. Elijah disguised himself as one of the princes and came to the king.

"Why are you angry, your majesty?" he asked the king. "This is certainly not plain dirt. Why would the Jewish people do anything so wicked as to get you angry? Maybe there is a secret in this dirt. Let us try to throw a little of it into the air. Perhaps it will turn into swords and arrows and we will be able to overcome the enemies of the king, just as it happened to Abraham, the father of the Jewish people."

"I have brought you a gift from the Jewish people."

Trust in God

The king thought for a minute and said, "You have spoken well! Let us try!" So they threw a little of the dirt into the air and behold! The dirt turned into swords and arrows! And with these weapons the king would conquer all his enemies.

The king was overjoyed and he said to Nachum Ish Gam-zu, "Please forgive me for being angry at you. You have brought me a very worthy gift indeed. Look, I will fill the box with gold and pearls instead of the wondrous soil that you have brought me. And please thank the Jewish people for me."

Nachum smiled. "I always said that everything is for the best!" he said. And so he took the box filled with precious stones and returned happily to the Land of Israel.

Source: Talmud Bavli, Ta'anith 21a

An uninterrupted prayer

A Jewish man went on a long journey. The man saw that it was time to say his prayers, but there was no synagogue to be found, and there were no houses anywhere around. There were only wide open spaces everywhere. So he stood up in the field at the side of the road and he prayed.

When he reached the "Shemoneh Esrey," a Roman nobleman passed by. (The Shemoneh Esrey is a prayer that you must say standing up, and you are not allowed to interrupt the prayer or speak in the middle of it.) The prince came riding on a horse, with his followers behind him, and his servants running ahead to clear the way for their master. All the people who came to meet the nobleman were always made to greet him and to honor him. They stood in fear of him, for they knew well that if they didn't bow down they would be punished severely.

The Roman saw the Jewish man standing in the field engrossed in prayer. So intently was he saying the Shemoneh Esrey that he did not look up

31 🌺

to see the prince who was approaching him. The prince impatiently called out a greeting, but the man did not answer. The prince was very angry, yet the man did not interrupt. The Jewish man had hardly finished when the prince shouted to him, "You fool! Do you not see me passing by here? How dare you not greet me! If I had hit you with my sword, who would have come to your rescue?" he exclaimed in anger. "I will punish you severely!"

"Please, please wait a minute!" pleaded the God-fearing man. "Perhaps if I explain what I was doing you will not be angry with me anymore," he said.

The Roman listened. "Tell me, your highness," asked the Jewish man. "Have you ever stood before the king?"

"Certainly," answered the nobleman proudly. "I have stood before the king many times!"

"If a simple man or even another prince should pass by while you are in the presence of the king and he should greet you, would you stop to answer him?" asked the Jewish man.

"Heaven forbid!" answered the Roman in awe. "It is not allowed. How can I speak to anyone when I am standing before the king? This would be a grave insult to his majesty!"

"What would the king do to you if you

The prince was very angry,
yet the man did not interrupt
his prayer

interrupted to greet someone?" asked the Jewish man.

"He would kill me with a sword," answered the prince.

"Do you see?" explained the man. "I was standing in prayer before the King of all kings, the Holy One, blessed be He! How could I stop to greet you?"

"You are right!" answered the prince. "I understand now why you did not greet me."

The Roman was not angry any more. He did not punish the man and allowed him to go on his journey in peace.

Source: Talmud Bavli, Berachoth 32b

2

The holy Temple

The holy Temple in its glory

hen the Holy Temple was standing in the sacred city of Jerusalem, there was not another building in the world to rival its magnificence. It was built of beautiful and sturdy stones. Part of it was covered over with blue-green marble that resembled the waves of the sea. All the gates were made of precious gold, and there was an altar covered with gold upon which incense was offered.

The Jewish people went up to the Holy Temple in Jerusalem three times a year; on Passover, on Shavuoth and on Sukkoth. From all the cities and towns and hamlets they came, and there was always room for everyone!

There were many courtyards in the Temple. The mothers and girls had a special courtyard which was called "the women's court." The holiest place of all was the "Holy of Holies." Two ark covers embroidered with gold thread were hung at the entrance. No one was allowed to enter the Holy of Holies except the High Priest on Yom Kippur.

There were thousands of candelabra in the

Holy Temple, all made of pure gold and decorated with golden flowers and buttons. The rest of the gold and silver vessels were so numerous that it was almost impossible to count them.

There was a vine in the Holy Temple, resembling a real vine with leaves and grapes, but it too was made of shimmering gold. Anyone who wanted to bring a gift to the Temple brought a leaf or a berry or a cluster of grapes made of gold and hung it on this vine. And the priests would come and gather these gifts and use them for many necessary repairs in the Holy Temple.

There were two special rooms in the Holy Temple; one room was for charity, and one room was for vessels. The charity room was called the "secret chamber" because good men brought money for the poor to that chamber. The poor people were given permission to go into the room and take as much of the money as they needed without anyone knowing it, so that they would not feel ashamed about taking charity.

The second room was called the chamber for vessels. If someone wanted to donate a vessel to the Holy Temple, he brought it to this room. The priests used the vessels that they needed for the sacred services in the Holy Temple.

There were three steps leading from the courtyard of Israel to the second courtyard, that of the priests, and above them was a platform where the

Levites stood singing from the Book of Psalms during the offerings.

The Levites had violins, flutes, cymbals, and many other ancient musical instruments which we no longer have today. Their songs and music were inspiring and wonderful.

On the six intermediate days of Sukkoth, during the celebration of the Drawing of the Water, the Levites stood on the fifteen steps that led from the womens' courtyard to that of Israel, and sang.

People from all over the world came to see the beauty and grandeur of the Holy Temple. The Jewish people loved it not only for its splendor. They loved it also because they prayed in the Temple to their Father in Heaven, to the Holy One, blessed be He. They brought their sacrifices to the Temple, and God answered their prayers. He forgave their sins and He sent them blessings without end. Whoever entered the Holy Temple came out contented and happy.

All this was when the Holy Temple was standing. And now that we have neither the Temple nor the Holy of Holies nor golden altars, where shall we pray?

Instead of the Holy Temple, we have synagogues. They are like small temples. There we pray and we ask God to forgive us and to send us a happy new year. We ask God to make all the sick people well, and to bring the Messiah soon. And if we are worthy, He will rebuild the Temple as of old and the new edifice will be even more beautiful and more splendid than the one which was destroyed.

Sources: Jerusalem Talmud, Shekalim, 5:4
Talmud Bavli, Sukkah, 48, 51
Talmud Bavli, Yoma, 38
Talmud Bavli, Tamid, 29
Talmud Bavli, Ta'anith, 33
Josephus, *The Wars of the Jews*, chapter 55
Josephus, *Antiquities*, chapter 8

Yom Kippur in the days of the holy Temple

ow was Yom Kippur celebrated in Jerusalem when the Holy Temple was still standing?

One week before Yom Kippur, the High Priest went to the Holy Temple. All the people of the city followed him. Men, women, and children came out of their homes and watched the High Priest walk to the Temple. It was a colorful procession.

First came the King and his sons clad in royal splendor, and then came the Levites. All of them wore blue robes of silk. The priests had flowing robes of white satin. Then came the singers, the musicians, the trumpeters, and all the people who performed any ritual in the Holy Temple. The gatekeepers who guarded the gates of the Temple and those who made repairs were next. Near the High Priest walked the rabbis and behind them there were again priests holding gold bars to make way for the crowd. Last came the High Priest with all the venerable old and respected priests.

They all prayed when they reached the Holy

Escorting the High Priest
to the holy Temple

Temple. The voices of prayer were so powerful that birds in flight almost fell from the heavens, trembling with fear.

All night the High Priest was kept awake by the voices of the other priests studying the Torah. When the day dawned he put on golden robes, and offered the first sacrifice which had to be offered on Yom Kippur. Before he went to the Holy of Holies, where only the High Priest was permitted, he changed his garments again. He looked like an angel of God in his splendid white robes. He prayed to God and asked Him to forgive the Jewish people and to inscribe them for a good year.

The Levites and the priests and all the people stood in silence from morning to night. They watched the ritual of the High Priest and did not say a word. And when the High Priest prayed and uttered the name of God, they all bowed down to the ground and called out: "Blessed be the name of the glory of His kingdom for ever and ever." Watching the High Priest, they did not become hungry or tired.

There was a red ribbon in the entrance to the courtyard of the Holy Temple. In the evening at the close of Yom Kippur, the people watched the red ribbon turn as white as snow, and then they knew that God had forgiven their sins. At night they did not go straight home to eat, but first they took flaming torches and escorted the High Priest

43

The holy Temple

home. Everyone was eager to come forward and greet him happily. All the windows were decorated with garlands of flowers, beautiful tapestries, and embroidered cloths. Fortunate were those who saw this magnificent sight!

Sources: Yom Kippur Machzor
Eliyahu Kitov, *The Book of Our Heritage*
Mishnah Yoma, 1-7

The celebration of the Drawing of Water

Our Sages of blessed memory said: "A person who has never seen the joy at the ceremony of the Drawing of the Water has never witnessed joy in his life." What was this celebration?

On the second night of the Festival of Sukkoth, all the people went to the Holy Temple. The sons of the priests climbed up on the ladders to the golden menorahs, filled the cups with oil and lighted the candelabra.

What illumination there was! The dazzling lights of the Holy Temple were bright enough to light all the courtyards of Jerusalem! The Levites played musical instruments and sang beautiful songs of praise to God.

The great sages, the teachers of the Torah, the head of the Court, and the elders all danced and sang. They held flaming torches in their hands, tossed them in the air and caught them again.

The head of the Sanhedrin (Rabbinic Court), Rabban Shimon ben Gamliel, skillfully juggled eight flaming torches at once, tossing them in the air and catching them in turn, without having them touch each other. And so they danced, sang and rejoiced all night.

At daybreak, two priests took silver horns and sounded them for all to hear. This was a signal for everyone to go to the Well of Shiloach, which was not far from the Holy Temple. At the well, the priests drew water and filled a golden bottle with the sweet waters of Shiloach. Then they formed a procession and, blowing their horns, they paraded back to the Holy Temple. In the Temple they took two goblets of silver. They filled one goblet with water which they had carried in the golden bottle. The second goblet they filled with sparkling wine. The water and the wine were poured on the altar in the Holy Temple.

The Levites again took up their musical instruments and played beautiful music with their violins, cymbals and lyres. The priests sounded their horns and the people bowed low. Then they circled the altar, with the lulav, myrtles, willows and ethrog in their hands.

When the ceremonies ended, they returned home and ate the festival meal amid much gladness and rejoicing.

Sources: Talmud Bavli, Sukkah 51b
Tosefta, 4

🌹 46

Rabban Shimon
ben Gamliel
skillfully juggling
eight flaming torches

Honoring Father
and Mother

Rabbi Tarfon
and his mother

any years ago, there lived a great rabbi. He was both wise and good. He had learned the entire Torah and many students came from afar to study with him.

People loved him for his great goodness and respected him for his great learning. His name was Rabbi Tarfon.

Rabbi Tarfon had an old mother. After a time his mother became ill, and she was so weak that she hardly had enough strength to take care of herself. Rabbi Tarfon's servants and his many disciples offered to help the old lady. But Rabbi Tarfon himself wanted to honor his ailing mother and to care for her. Every time she wished to get in or out of bed, he ran, bent down to the floor and let his mother put her feet on his back to climb into bed. He did the same to help her out of bed.

It happened one Sabbath that the sick old mother was feeling a little better. She called Rabbi Tarfon and said to him, "Tarfon, my son, I would like to go out to our courtyard for a short walk."

51 🙚

Honoring Father and Mother

Rabbi Tarfon was very happy that his mother was well enough to get up and to take a walk outside. After being confined to her room for so many days, the old mother enjoyed the fresh air. She was warmed by the bright sun, and she was delighted with the many flowers and the song of the birds. But suddenly, right in the middle of her walk, the strap of her sandal tore, and she remained standing on her bare foot. Rabbi Tarfon was worried.

"My mother can't walk with her sandal torn," he thought, "and we can't get it repaired on the Sabbath. How will mother return home? I can't let her walk barefooted. She is so old and frail. She might catch a cold stepping on the cold ground without a shoe on."

Then he had an idea. He got down to the ground, stretched out his hands, and allowed his mother to walk on his hands rather than on the cold ground. Thus she got home safely and lay down to rest.

Some time later, Rabbi Tarfon became ill. When the rabbis, his friends, came to visit him, his old mother told them, "Please pray for my son, Rabbi Tarfon, for he accords me too much respect."

"What unusual kindness did he show you?" asked the rabbis.

The old mother told them the story of her torn

sandal and how her son had let her walk on his hands.

On hearing the story, the rabbis said, "That was a fine thing to do. But even if he had done a thousand times as much for you, it wouldn't come close to the honor that the Torah intended in the commandment: Honor your father and your mother.

Sources: Jerusalem Talmud, Peah, chapter 1
Talmud Bavli, Kiddushin, 31b

Respect for a father

The High Priest of the Holy Temple in Jerusalem had beautiful robes, with a breast-plate studded with precious, sparkling jewels. It once happened that one of the rare jewels, a jasper, fell off and was lost. So the great rabbis of Israel took many coins of gold to buy another precious stone to replace the lost one. They went to many cities and said to many people, "We need a jewel that is big and beautiful for the robe of the High Priest. Do any of you know where we can buy a precious stone?" But no one could help them.

At last they met a man who told them, "In the city of Ashkelon there is a wealthy man named Dama ben Nethina. He has the most beautiful gems and pearls in the land."

So the rabbis went straight to the home of Dama ben Nethina in Ashkelon and knocked on his door. Dama came out, and seeing the honored visitors, said to them politely, "Welcome great rabbis! What is it you want? Is there anything I can do for you?"

The wise rabbis answered, "We have heard that you have precious stones, and we want to buy a jasper from you. Will you agree to sell us the jewel? We have many coins of gold that we brought with us. We will give you one hundred of them for the precious stone."

Dama ben Nethina listened and said, "Very well, I will gladly sell you the precious stone. Please come into my house and wait just a minute. I will bring you what you asked for right away."

Dama went to the box in which he kept precious jewels, and to his dismay he found that the box was locked and the keys were gone! Dama looked everywhere and finally went into his father's bedroom. He saw his father fast asleep on his bed, and the keys to the box lay there, under his pillow.

Dama stopped and thought to himself, "I might wake up my father if I pull the keys from under the pillow. Perhaps he will get frightened at being awakened suddenly. No, I cannot wake father from his deep sleep!"

Dama returned to the rabbis who were waiting, and he said quietly, "I cannot sell you the precious stone because my father has the keys to the box of jewels, and he is asleep."

The rabbis thought that Dama had found an excuse because he wanted more money for the precious stone, so they said, "If you will sell us the

55 🌹

*"I cannot sell you the precious stone
because my father has the keys and he is asleep."*

stone, we will give you two hundred coins of gold instead of the one hundred we promised!"

But Dama was determined. "No, I cannot wake up my father!" he said.

"We need the jewel very badly. We will be glad to pay you three hundred gold coins for it," insisted the rabbis.

But Dama ben Nethina refused. Even when the rabbis offered him one thousand pieces of gold, he would not change his mind. "I will not wake up father for all the money in the world," he declared.

When the rabbis realized that Dama would not sell them the jewel, they went away, very disappointed.

Soon after, Dama ben Nethina's father woke up from his sleep. Dama took the keys and opened the jewel box. He took out the precious stone, and hurried to find the great rabbis of Israel. When he caught up with the wise men and gave them the precious stone, their disappointment turned to joy. They wanted to pay him the thousand gold pieces which they had offered him before they left his house, but Dama would not accept the offer.

"Pay me one hundred pieces of gold," he said to them, "as you offered me at the beginning. I don't want to be paid for honoring my father."

The rabbis smiled and said, "Let us go and see how Dama ben Nethina honors his father. We can all learn a great lesson from him!"

Honoring Father and Mother

Sources: Jerusalem Talmud, Pe'ah, chapter 1
Talmud Bavli, Kiddushin, 31a

Rabbi Yehoshua
and the butcher

very wise man lived in the Land of Israel and his name was Rabbi Yehoshua. Everyone called him "the light of Israel" because he enlightened the whole world with his wisdom and his knowledge of Torah.

One night Rabbi Yehoshua had a dream. In his dream he heard a voice saying, "How fortunate you are, Rabbi Yehoshua! When you come to Paradise, you will dwell together with Nannas the butcher, because his portion in Paradise is equal to your portion."

Rabbi Yehoshua awoke from his sleep and thought, "How amazing! All my life I have studied Torah and obeyed the commandments. I have eighty students to whom I teach Torah from morning till night, but in the end my portion is the same as Nannas the butcher's, who is certainly a crude and simple man!"

Rabbi Yehoshua was dismayed. In the morning he called his students and said to them, "Let us go and look for Nannas the butcher, because I want to get to know the man who will be my companion in Paradise."

Rabbi Yehoshua and his disciples went from city to city and from village to village, and everywhere he asked, "Does Nannas the butcher live here?"

At last he came to a city and the people told him, "Nannas the butcher? Yes, he lives in this city. But what do you want of him? You are very wise and very righteous. What do you want of a man as simple as Nannas?"

But Rabbi Yehoshua repeated his request. "Please, would you invite him to come to see me?" So the people went to the butcher and said to him, "Rabbi Yehoshua has asked that you come to see him immediately."

Nannas thought that they were mocking him. "You are making fun of me! How is it possible that the great and wise rabbi should want to speak to me? I will not go," he declared. "You only want to embarrass me!"

The people returned to Rabbi Yehoshua with the reply, "Nannas does not want to come to you! Now you can see that it is not proper for you to speak to a person as unworthy as he."

But Rabbi Yehoshua himself went to the butcher. When Nannas saw Rabbi Yehoshua, he was very awed by the great man. He bowed before him and asked, "Why has the rabbi come to visit

Rabbi Yehoshua went to see Nannas the butcher

me? How do I deserve such a great honor? You are so righteous and so wise. Everyone calls you the light of Israel, while I am just a simple, un-educated butcher."

Rabbi Yehoshua then spoke to Nannas. "Tell me, what are some of your activities? What do you do when you are not in the butcher shop?"

Nannas replied, "I have an old father and mother. They are sick and helpless. Every day I dress them, feed them and wash them, and I do all I can for them."

Rabbi Yehoshua stood up, kissed him on the head, and said, "How sweet and how pleasant are your deeds! You honor your father and your mother, just as the Holy Torah commands, 'Honor your father and your mother.' How fortunate am I that I am worthy to be your companion in Paradise!"

Source: Seder haDoroth

Mother and father
are best of all

here once lived an old man and his wife. They loved the ways of the Torah and they admired all the children who studied it. But the man and his wife were very sad because they had no children of their own to study Torah.

Every day the old man would go out to meet the children at the close of school. Lovingly he would say, "Tell me, my dear children, what did you learn today?"

And when the children recited to him all they had learned, he would utter a deep sigh and whisper, "How lucky are your parents who have children to study the Torah! I am so sorry that I don't have any children to learn the words of the Holy Torah."

The old man gave his money to scholars so that they could sit and study the Torah all day. Now they did not have to interrupt their studies by going to work to earn a living.

The Holy One, blessed be He, saw how much the fine old man loved the Torah and those who

"Tell me, dear children,
what did you learn today?"

study it. He took pity on him and granted him a son. A beautiful little boy was born to him. How delighted were the parents, and how they loved him!

When the little boy grew older, his father took him on his shoulders one day, and brought him to school. The journey was long, and the school was very far away. When they reached the school at last, the father met the teacher. "Please teach the Torah to my little boy," he said.

The teacher agreed to include the boy among his students. The little boy joined all the children in the study of the first book of the Bible, Genesis.

From that day on, the father would bring his son to school every day. The child loved to study and in a short time he knew the first stories of Creation.

One day the little boy said to the old man, "Father, why do you tire yourself carrying me on your shoulders? Please let me go to school by myself!" His father reluctantly agreed. "Go my son," he said. "Go in peace!" And so the boy took his books and went off to school all alone. He had hardly gone half the distance when a horseman passed by. He was one of the nobles of the king who ruled the land at that time.

When the nobleman saw the handsome little boy, he said to himself, "I will snatch him and he will be mine!" And so he did. He grabbed the

65 🌸

child, put him on his horse, and fled with him to the king's palace.

That afternoon the old man and woman waited for their little boy to return from school. They waited and waited. It was getting late and the child was not home. The father ran to the school frantically and asked the teacher, "Where is my little boy? Why hasn't he returned home yet?"

The teacher was surprised. "Your little boy was not in school at all today," he said.

When the wretched father heard this, he started to sob inconsolably, and he went all over town looking for his son. He asked everyone he met, "Have you seen my little boy?" But no one had seen him. His mother, too, searched for the child everywhere, and she was grieved and distressed beyond all measure.

God saw their sorrow, and He pitied the poor parents. That very evening He caused the king to become ill. The king felt very sick, and lying on the bed, he said to his servants, "Bring me the book of medicine, and I will try to read about a remedy for my illness."

"Bring the book of medicine!" a servant was commanded.

The book was brought, and God wrought a miracle. The book of medicine was changed into the Book of Genesis. The king took the book and wanted to read it, but alas, he did not understand a word, because he did not know any Hebrew. The servants said to the king, "It appears that this is a Jewish book. We will look for a Jewish man and he will be able to read it to you."

They searched, but they could not find anyone to read the book. Then came the same nobleman who had snatched the child that morning, and he said to the king, "This morning I passed through a Jewish town and I took a child from there. Perhaps he will know how to read this book."

Immediately the child was brought to the king. "Can you read this book?" the king asked him. The little boy recognized the Book of Genesis, the same book he had studied in school. Remembering school, he started to cry.

The king was startled. "What is the matter, my sweet lad? Are you afraid of me?"

"No," answered the little boy. "I am not afraid. But I remembered my dear father who had asked the teacher to teach me the Torah, and this is the book I studied. Yes, I can read this book very well."

The little boy read to the king and explained all there was in it. By the time the king heard how God created the world, he was strong enough to sit up in a chair. And when the boy finished reading the portion about sanctifying the Sabbath, the king had completely recovered.

"If you agree to stay with me, I will give you

whatever your heart desires. All the toys and all the sweets in the world will be yours, because it is through your efforts that I became well," said the king.

But the boy answered, "I ask for nothing, only to allow me to return to my mother and father. They are, no doubt, very sad because I did not return home. I will never be happy without my mother and father."

The king replied, "I see that you are a very good lad, and that you love your parents more than the gifts I promised you. You may return home, and take whatever you desire as a gift from me."

The boy selected beautiful gifts for his father and mother, and then he was returned home in a golden coach. His parents were overjoyed when they saw their son again. They thanked God for His help, and they lived in peace and happiness ever after.

Source: Midrash Assereth Hadibroth

🌹 68

4

Respect for people

Kamtza
and Bar-Kamtza

nsult and revenge caused the burning of our Holy Temple and the destruction of Jerusalem. It happened this way:

At the time of the Temple, there were many men of great wealth in Jerusalem. One of these wealthy men planned a great feast in honor of a happy occasion. The man invited all his friends and acquaintances to come share the feast with him — to eat, drink and rejoice.

Now the rich man had a good friend named Kamtza whom he liked very much, so he said to his servant, "Go to my good friend, Kamtza, and invite him to my feast."

The servant was not paying close attention and he did not hear the name of the friend clearly. So he went to another man who had a similar name, Bar-Kamtza, and he said to him, "My master would like you to come to a great feast he has prepared."

But Bar-Kamtza was not a friend of the rich man at all. On the contrary! The rich man did not

71 🌺

like Bar-Kamtza and always quarreled with him. So Bar-Kamtza was very surprised at the invitation and thought to himself, "Why did the man invite me? We are not even friends!" Then he added with satisfaction, "Perhaps he wants to make peace with me. If that's the case, I will not be angry with him any more. I will go to his party."

Bar-Kamtza put on his best clothes and went to the house of the rich man. He sat down at the table among the other invited guests. How wonderful it would be, he thought, if the rich man really wanted to make up with him.

But not so! When the rich man walked about greeting his guests, he looked among them for his good friend, Kamtza. But do you know whom he saw? Bar-Kamtza, of course! He became angry and ran to him shouting, "What are you doing here? *You who hate me.* Get up at once and leave my house!"

Bar-Kamtza was humiliated. Imagine being chased from the house in front of all the guests! His face pale and his voice trembling, he whispered, "It seems that I was invited by mistake. But since I am already here, please allow me to stay, and I will pay you for my food and drink."

But the host shouted even more harshly, "No! I will not have you! Go now!"

Bar-Kamtza begged him. "Allow me to stay just this once. I will pay for half your feast."

"Get up at once and leave my house!"

"No, No," insisted the other man. "I do not want your pay! Leave my house at once!"

Bar-Kamtza pleaded with his host, offering to pay for the whole feast. But the rich man would not hear of it. He seized Bar-Kamtza, pulled him up by force and chased him out of his house.

Bar-Kamtza was very angry. The rich man had so openly insulted him before all those guests. Yet no one came to his aid; not one man asked the rich man to allow him to remain in the house.

"I will take revenge on them all!" declared Bar-Kamtza in his anger. "The host will be sorry about this, and all his guests will regret that they did not help me! Their houses will be burned to the ground!" Bar-Kamtza forgot that he also would be hurt because if all the houses burned, his house would be among them.

What did he do? He went to the king of the Romans, who then ruled over Israel, and said to him, "O king, I want to reveal a secret to you. The Jews of Jerusalem are planning a rebellion against you! They do not want you to be the ruler over them. They are asking for another king!"

The king became angry and sent a mighty army against Jerusalem. The Roman soldiers came to Jerusalem, burned the Holy Temple and destroyed the whole city.

Source: Talmud Bavli, Gittin, 55-56

Respect
for human beings

There was a scholar named Shimon the son of Elazar, who studied in a yeshiva (a Torah school) for many years and became a great rabbi.

One day Rabbi Shimon decided to return home to see his father and mother. He bought a donkey and started out on the journey to his birthplace.

The journey was a long one. The donkey trotted slowly, and Rabbi Shimon sat in peace, absorbed in his thoughts. "How fortunate I am to have learned so much Torah! When I come home, many students will want to study with me. They will want me to be their teacher."

Rabbi Shimon was very pleased and very proud of his great learning.

On the road, a man approached him. The man was ugly and his clothes were dirty. He had a curious expression on his face, and all his movements were strange. Rabbi Shimon had never before seen a man who looked so unpleasant, and he felt uncomfortable in his presence. The wanderer turned to Rabbi Shimon and called out

in a gruff coarse voice, "Greetings, rabbi." Rabbi
Shimon was annoyed that someone so lowly should
disturb his thoughts. This man, he thought, was
acting without any manners, indeed with impu-
dence. Perhaps he even meant to insult him. Not
only did his face seem ugly, but his behavior as
well. So instead of returning a friendly greeting,
Rabbi Shimon exclaimed, "You fool! How plain
you are! Are all the people in your town as homely
as you are?"

The man was very insulted and answered, "I
don't know. But if you don't like my appearance,
please go to the craftsman who made me and tell
him: How ugly is the vessel that You fashioned!"

Rabbi Shimon thought, "Who is the craftsman
who made this man? Surely, God Who created all
men. Alas, what have I done to speak so foolishly?"

Rabbi Shimon was now very sorry about his
angry outburst. He got down from his donkey,
bowed low before the man and begged, "Forgive
me for speaking so rudely to you. Please do not be
angry at me anymore." But the man refused to
hear Rabbi Shimon's pleas and said, "I will not
forgive you until you go to my Maker and tell Him
how ugly His creature is."

Having spoken, the man turned his back on
Rabbi Shimon and did not even want to glance in
his direction.

Rabbi Shimon walked after the man the entire

The man called out in a gruff coarse voice, "Greetings, Rabbi."

way, begging to be forgiven, but the man would not be appeased. At last they came to the city. Many people were waiting to welcome the rabbi. When they saw him, they rushed forward and called, "Shalom! Welcome, our Rabbi, our teacher!"

On seeing this, the wayfarer asked the city people, "Whom do you call our teacher and our rabbi?"

The townspeople answered, "This man, Rabbi Shimon the son of Elazar, the great sage and scholar. He is returning to our city after many years of study."

The man answered bitterly, "If such a man as he is a rabbi and a sage, I pray that there be no more like him in Israel!"

The people were shocked at his words, and asked him to explain. So the man told them all that happened: how he had greeted the rabbi, and how Rabbi Shimon had insulted him.

"Please forgive him in spite of what he did, for the sake of his great learning," replied the people of the city.

The man agreed and said, "I forgive him only for your sake, only because you have asked me to do so. Perhaps he will learn not to behave in such a manner again."

Rabbi Shimon was very happy that the man had forgiven his insult. He went at once to the house of study (synagogue) to teach Torah to the townspeople. And what was the first lesson he taught them?

"A man should always be as pliable as a reed, and never as hard as a cedar tree. A man must be pleasant to everyone. He must speak softly and gently, and not be boastful and arrogant. For a proud man is like a hard tree, and anyone stumbling on him gets hurt."

After this, Rabbi Shimon was careful not to insult anyone ever again.

Sources: Talmud Bavli, Ta'anith 20a-b
Avoth de Rabbi Nathan, chapter 41

Rabbi Elazar
and the Roman

group of Jews went on a pilgrimage to the holy Temple in Jerusalem. Among them was the great and wise man whose name was Elazar ben Shamua. The pilgrims walked for a time along the sea coast, and from afar, they saw a ship sailing slowly in the middle of the ocean.

Suddenly, a great storm arose. The waves dashed against the ship, tossing it up and down with great fury. Soon the ship was smashed and it sank to the bottom of the sea. All the people aboard were drowned. Only one man remained alive. He held on to one of the boards of the shipwrecked vessel and swam until he reached land.

The man had no clothes, for he had cast them into the sea to lighten the load in order to make swimming easier. When he saw people walking along the seashore, he hid behind a rock because he was without clothes. Only his head was visible as he called out to them, "Please have pity, good people, and give me some clothes to put on. My ship sank in the ocean and I was left with nothing to wear!''

The people recognized the man to be one of the cruel Romans who ruled over Israel in those days. They did not want to help him, for they were made to suffer greatly under Roman rule. They laughed at the Roman and said to him, "May the same misfortune befall all of your people!''

The Roman stood there in confusion, not knowing what to do. Suddenly, he saw Rabbi Elazar ben Shamua in the group and realized by the manner in which everyone treated him that he must be an important man. He turned to Rabbi Elazar and said, "I see that you are an old and respected man. You surely know how to treat people. Have pity on me, I beg you, and lend me any clothes you can spare.''

Rabbi Elazar immediately took off his coat and gave it to the man. Then he brought him home and gave him food to eat and a place to rest, for the man was tired and hungry. He also gave him some money and a horse to ride, and finally accompanied him politely for a long stretch of the journey.

Many years later the same shipwrecked Roman became king. All this time he remembered how some Jewish people had laughed at him in his trouble. Now he wanted revenge for the unkindness. So he wrote a letter to the commander of his army saying, "You are to slay all the Jews in the Land of Israel!"

When the Jewish people heard about this terrible edict, they were worried and frightened. They came to Rabbi Elazar ben Shamua and said, "Please go to the king and ask him to forgive us. Take plenty of gold as a gift to him." Rabbi Elazar agreed to go on the mission, taking plenty of gold with him.

When he arrived at the gates of the palace, he told the guards, "Please tell the king that a Jewish man is at the gate and wants to see the king!" The guards did as they were asked.

"Let him come in at once!" ordered the king.

Recognizing Rabbi Elazar as he entered, the king clearly remembered the kindness Rabbi Elazar had shown him in time of need. He jumped up and bowed to him saying, "Welcome, Rabbi. What is your wish here? Perhaps I can help you in some way. Why have you come such a long way? What is it that brings you from afar?"

Rabbi Elazar explained the reason for his coming, and asked the king to excuse the Jews for not showing kindness long ago.

"They did not do as your Torah commands," the king said angrily. "They not only failed to help me, but they also laughed at me. Therefore, I will kill them!"

"Please forgive my people, even if they did not

"Please tell the king that a Jewish man is at the gate."

treat you kindly," said Rabbi Elazar. He held out the gold to the king. "Here is a fine present that they have sent you," he said.

The king heard Rabbi Elazar's plea and said, "I don't need the present. But I will forgive them for your sake. Take back the gold. I give it to you in return for the money which you lent me then. Please go into my treasure house and select seventy beautiful garments for the coat that you gave me many years ago, and go back to your home in peace."

The Jewish people rejoiced when Rabbi Elazar returned to the Land of Israel and told them that the king forgave them.

Everyone thanked Rabbi Elazar ben Shamua. The people knew that they were saved only because of his good deeds long ago.

Source: Midrash Koheleth Rabbah, chapter 11

5

The honesty of our Sages

Rabbi Pinchas ben Yair and the poor

Many years ago, there lived a wise and righteous man in the Land of Israel. His name was Pinchas ben Yair. He was well-known for his great goodness and wisdom, and many people turned to him for advice.

Once, two poor men came to the city in which Rabbi Pinchas ben Yair lived. They went from house to house to ask for alms. But the people of the city were poor themselves and couldn't help the men very much. Each person gave them some grains of barley so they could grind it into flour and bake bread to eat. In this way, they gathered two small bags of barley.

Finally, one of the poor men said to his friend, "Perhaps we ought to go to a neighboring city. We might be luckier there."

His friend agreed, but since they didn't want to carry the barley which they had already gathered, they brought it to Rabbi Pinchas ben Yair for safekeeping.

"Please keep this barley for a few days. When

we return from the other city, we will come and get it."

Rabbi Pinchas ben Yair agreed to keep the barley for the poor men, and they went on their way. But in the neighboring city they met with no better luck, and they decided to go to another city and still another. As for the barley, they forgot all about it.

Rabbi Pinchas ben Yair waited a few days, a week, a month but the poor men did not return. A year passed, and Rabbi Pinchas said, "If I leave the barley in my storehouse any longer, it will spoil or maybe the mice will eat it up. When these wretched men return nothing will be left of it."

So Rabbi Pinchas ben Yair went out into the field. He plowed the soil and then he sowed the grains of barley. The rains came, the seeds sprouted and new barley grew abundantly. When the grain ripened, Rabbi Pinchas ben Yair cut it and stuffed it in bigger sacks, for by now there was much more grain than the two men had collected at first. Then he left the sacks in his shed for the poor men.

But the men did not return that year either, and Rabbi Pinchas sowed the seeds and harvested the grain again. This time there was even more barley which he stuffed into still bigger sacks.

Every year Rabbi Pinchas plowed and sowed, cut and threshed the grain. Finally he built a

"Please keep this barley for a few days . . ."

threshing floor for all the barley he had.

Seven years passed. The two men happened by chance to return to the same city at last. They were very poor. Then one of them remembered that they had left some barley at the home of Rabbi Pinchas ben Yair. "Perhaps the barley is still good," thought the poor men. "Even if it isn't fresh, it will still be better than nothing at all."

The men came to Rabbi Pinchas and asked, "Can you return the barley which we left with you seven years ago?"

Rabbi Pinchas recognized the poor men and greeted them happily. "Certainly, I will return the grain to you, but you won't be able to carry it yourself. Bring donkeys and camels and pick up all of your barley."

Saying this, he took them to the threshing floor and pointed to the huge pile of grain. "All this came out of your two bags of barley."

Rabbi Pinchas handed them all the sacks of grain without asking any reward for his years of toil and hard work. The men thanked him, ate their fill and then sold the rest of the grain, so that they never had to beg for alms again.

Source: Midrash Devarim Rabbah, chapter 83

Honesty

Rabbi Shimon ben Shetach was a man of great wisdom who had many disciples. He did not want to accept pay from his pupils, for our Sages, may their memory be blessed, said, "Just as the Holy One, blessed be He, gave the Torah to the children of Israel without pay, so we must teach Torah to others." Therefore, he tried to earn his bread by engaging in trade. He would buy flax from which to make threads for clothing, and he would carry it to market himself to sell to others.

His pupils saw that this work was difficult for Rabbi Shimon ben Shetach, and they said to him, "Rabbi, please let us lighten your hard work. We will buy a strong, healthy donkey for you, to carry the flax on its back."

Rabbi Shimon agreed to their suggestion, and they hurried to find a donkey for their teacher. Soon they met an Arab who had the kind of donkey they wanted.

"Would you want to sell us your donkey?" they asked the Arab.

"Yes, if you pay me a good price."

The disciples paid the Arab the price that he had asked, and they started on the way back to their teacher. On the way home, they stopped to examine the donkey carefully, and lo and behold — a surprise! On the rope tied around the donkey's neck hung a precious stone which they had not noticed when they bought the donkey.

The pupils were happy, for now their teacher would be rich enough not to have to work. He would be able to study the Torah all day, and to teach without any toil or worry.

When they came to Rabbi Shimon, they called out with joy, "Rabbi, from now on you won't have to wear yourself out with hard work. You are rich now!"

Rabbi Shimon was astonished. "Why?" he asked.

"We have bought a donkey from an Arab, and there was a precious stone hung from its neck," continued the pupils. "Sell it and you will have enough money to live comfortably for a long time."

"Did the Arab know that a precious stone was hung on the donkey's neck?" asked Rabbi Shimon.

"No," answered the pupils.

Rabbi Shimon smiled and said, "I purchased a donkey, but I did not buy the precious stone." And he promptly went and returned the precious stone to the Arab. The Arab was surprised at the honesty

The disciples paid the Arab, and started on the
way back to their teacher

of Rabbi Shimon ben Shetach and exclaimed, "Blessed is the God of the Jewish people, who commanded to return a loss to its owner. Blessed are those who believe in Him and who observe His commandments!"

Rabbi Shimon ben Shetach was satisfied. "The blessings of the God of Israel from the lips of an Arab are far sweeter to me than all the precious stones in the world," he said.

Source: Jerusalem Talmud, Bava Metzia, chapter 2

The return of
something lost

here once lived a queen in the city of Rome. She had a splendid palace, and much gold and silver.

While taking a walk one day, the queen discovered that her jewels were gone. She had lost a ring decorated with diamonds, a string of pearls and a beautiful gold bracelet. The queen was very upset over her lost jewelry because she prized them above all her possessions.

A messenger was sent through the streets of Rome, proclaiming, "The queen has lost some precious jewels. A generous reward awaits the person who returns them within thirty days! But whoever keeps the jewels beyond thirty days will be punished by death!"

The queen hoped that the finder would quickly return the lost articles. But in vain.

The great Rabbi Shmuel bar Susrati came to Rome about that time. And it happened that while he was walking in the street, he found the queen's lost jewels. Rabbi Shmuel kept the jewels, and only after thirty days did he go to the queen. "Here

95 🌹

are your jewels, O Queen! I have found them!" he said.

The queen stared at Rabbi Shmuel in amazement. Indeed, she was happy that her jewels were found. But at the same time, she was angry that Rabbi Shmuel hadn't returned them sooner.

The queen saw that Rabbi Shmuel was a wise old man, and thought that he had perhaps not kept her jewels intentionally. So she asked him, "Have you just come to Rome?"

"No," he replied, "I have been here about thirty days."

"Have you heard the proclamation about my lost jewels?" she asked.

"Yes," replied Rabbi Shmuel calmly.

"Then perhaps you did not understand it. Repeat to me what you heard," ordered the queen.

Rabbi Shmuel repeated the proclamation. "They said that the person who returns the jewels within thirty days will get a reward. But the one who hides them will be punished severely."

The queen said in surprise, "In that case, I do not understand you at all. If you were here and you heard the proclamation clearly, and you understood what it said, why didn't you return the jewels right away?"

Rabbi Shmuel answered the queen. "I shall gladly explain the reason. I did not want you to think that I returned your jewels in order to earn

"Here are your jewels, O Queen!"

the reward, or because I am afraid of you. I returned them because in the Torah, the Lord our God commanded us to return a lost article to its owner."

The queen realized that Rabbi Shmuel was an honest and righteous man, and she said, "Blessed is the Lord, the God of Israel." After that, she always accorded honor and respect to Rabbi Shmuel.

Source: Jerusalem Talmud, Bava Metzia, chapter 2

The lost chickens

Once a man was walking along the road, carrying some chickens with him. After a while the load became heavy, and he sat down on the doorstep of the home of Rabbi Chanina ben Dosa. He put down the hens, and thought to himself, "I will leave my chickens here for a short time while I go to buy food. Then I will come back to get them."

The man went to the food store, and returning to reclaim his chickens, he forgot where he had left them. He searched and searched, but he could not find them. Sad and disappointed, the man continued on his journey.

In the meantime, the hens became hungry and started cackling. Inside the house, the wife of Rabbi Chanina ben Dosa heard the noise and went to the yard to investigate. She found the hens in her doorway, their legs tied. The woman looked everywhere, but she could not find the owner. So she took the chickens home and showed them to Rabbi Chanina ben Dosa.

Rabbi Chanina said, "Someone left these hens

*He sat down on the doorstep
of Rabbi Chanina ben Dosa*

here, and forgot where he put them. We will take care of them until he comes to claim them. In the meantime, we must give them food to eat and water to drink. Only we will not use the eggs."

And so they did. Seeds were scattered and a dish was filled with water. The chickens ate their fill, walked about the yard, laid eggs and warmed them. The eggs hatched into chicks. The chicks grew into hens and roosters. So it went — the chickens laid eggs; the eggs hatched; and soon the yard was filled with hens and chicks.

Rabbi Chanina saw that raising chickens was becoming too difficult a task for him. He was poor and hardly had enough food for his household. Where would he get feed for so many chickens? They were a nuisance, too. The hens disturbed his rest by their constant cackling. They pecked at the vegetables in his garden and they flew in through the window and soiled the house.

Rabbi Chanina ben Dosa found a solution. He sold all the hens and chicks, and with the money he bought goats. He reasoned, "The goats will go out to pasture, and I won't have to feed them."

So each morning the goats would go out to graze, and every evening they returned to the barn.

Some years later, the man who had left the chickens was passing through town. When he saw the house of Rabbi Chanina ben Dosa, he remembered the place, and he said to the friend who was with him, "This is the house at which I once left my chickens. I never found them because I could not remember the place."

Rabbi Chanina ben Dosa overheard the conversation. He looked out the window and spoke to the man. "Do you have a mark by which you can prove that the hens were yours? Can you remember the color of their feathers? Do you know what kind of cord you had tied around their feet?"

The man replied, "The hens were brown and I had them tied with red cord."

Rabbi Chanina was satisfied. He brought the man to the barn and showed him the goats. Then he explained, "These goats belong to you. I bought them after selling the chickens which you left at my doorstep."

The man thanked Rabbi Chanina ben Dosa and happily returned home with his goats.

Source: Talmud Bavli, Ta'anith 25

Integrity

Rav Safra was a wise man. Torah and prayers occupied all his days, except for the few hours he spent in his store selling his wares to earn enough money for food and clothing.

Some customers came to his store one day and asked, "Do you have some fine cloth to sell us?"

"Yes," said Rav Safra, and he showed them the goods.

The customers liked the cloth. "How much is it?" they asked.

"Ten coins," replied Rav Safra.

"Ten coins! That is too expensive!" complained the customers. "We will pay you only five coins."

Rav Safra shook his head. "No, I cannot sell this fine cloth for only five coins," he said.

The people left without buying the goods. That night they thought: "Too bad that we didn't buy the cloth. It is really worth the ten coins that Rav Safra asked for it. Tomorrow morning we will go back and buy it."

The customers liked the cloth.
"How much is it?"

And at home, Rav Safra thought: "I am sorry that I didn't sell the cloth for five coins. True, it is a very low price, but I need the money very badly! If they return tomorrow, I shall sell it for five coins."

The following morning the customers came to Rav Safra. "Greetings," they said. "We have come back for the cloth that we wanted to buy last night."

But at that moment, Rav Safra was standing in prayer, reciting the "Shema," and he could not interrupt to reply. When he finished his prayers, the customers repeated their offer.

"We have returned to buy the cloth for ten coins. We will pay you the price you asked for in the beginning," they said.

"No. I had already made up my mind to sell it to you for five coins," said Rav Safra. "I will not accept any more."

The people admired his honesty. "Rav Safra is truly a righteous man," they said.

Source: She'iltoth de Rabbi Achai Gaon

6

A love of people

Aharon
the peace-maker

haron the Priest, the brother of Moshe, was much beloved by all the people. He never lost his temper and never scolded anyone. Even when he knew that a man had done wrong, he never said to him, "Wicked man, what evil you have done!" On the contrary! When he met anyone who had done wrong, he greeted him just as politely as if nothing happened. The man would walk away saying to himself, "How will I ever be able to face him? If only he knew what wicked things I have done, he would certainly not greet me. He wouldn't want to speak to me at all. He would not even look at me!" And when such a man was tempted to return to his wicked ways, he would remember Aharon — and refrain from doing evil.

It happened at times that people quarreled, and, in their anger, they refused to speak to one another.

What did Aharon do?

He sat down with the first man and said to him,

A love of people

"Do you know that I saw your friend, the one with whom you quarreled? He is very sorry that he made you angry. The poor fellow! He is beside himself with regret. He says: 'I am at fault. I infuriated my friend. How ashamed I am that I quarreled with him!' "

And so did Aharon speak to the man until his anger left him. He persisted until he felt that the man loved his friend as well as he had before the argument.

Then Aharon went to the second man and reasoned with him. "I was just visiting your friend, and I saw how much he loves you. He is upset that you are so angry with him. He says, 'I take the blame for getting my friend angry. I am ashamed to have done this to him. I wish he were my friend again.' "

And so Aharon spoke to the second man until he was willing to make peace with his friend.

When the two met the following day, they would embrace one another, and again they were good friends as before.

Thus, Aharon settled quarrels so that peace would prevail among the Jewish people. And the people loved him for this.

Sources: Avoth de Rabbi Nathan, chapter 12
Yalkut Shimoni, Chukkath

and again they were good friends as before .

The patience of Hillel

illel was of the family of King David, and he was himself a Nasi, or prince in Israel. There was not another man more wise and more respected in his time. Great sages came to counsel with him. Many disciples came to study with him. And never once did Hillel become haughty or impatient. He spoke lovingly and patiently to every man.

Once, two men were chatting about the Nasi. One of them said, "The aged Hillel does not get angry at anyone or anything."

The other man said, "I will irritate him so that he will become angry and scold me in anger."

"I can't believe that you will be able to do that," said the first. "I am ready to make a bet with you. If you really get Hillel angry, I will pay you four hundred coins of silver."

His friend laughed and said, "The money is mine already, for I know how I can make him angry."

This was on Friday. The aged Hillel was busy with preparations for welcoming the Sabbath. He was bathing and washing his head when he heard a clatter at the door.

"Which one here is Hillel? Which one here is Hillel?" shouted a shrill voice.

Another person might have certainly become angry at the rude man, shouting outside as if he didn't know where Hillel the Nasi lived. And to disturb him while bathing! How impudent the man was!

But not Hillel. "Perhaps the man wants to ask an important question about the Torah, and I must answer him immediately," he thought.

Hillel got dressed hurriedly and went outside. Quietly, he asked the man, "My son, what do you want?"

"I have a question to ask you," the man said.

"Ask your question, my son," said Hillel.

The man asked a silly question only to anger Hillel.

"Why do the Babylonians have egg-shaped heads?" And while he was speaking, he thought, "Hillel will surely become angry to be disturbed so before the Sabbath, when he is especially busy."

But Hillel answered gently. "My son, you have asked a very important question. The reason for their egg-shaped heads is that the midwives in Babylonia don't know how to handle new-born babies."

The man left and waited long enough for Hillel

113

to return to his Sabbath preparations. Then he returned to Hillel's house and shouted, "Which one here is Hillel? Which one here is Hillel?"

Hillel did not get angry. He dressed in a hurry, and greeted the man again.

"My son, what is it you want?"

"I have a question," said the man in a gruff voice.

Hillel said gently, "Ask your question, my son."

Again, the man asked a question which seemed rather silly.

"Why do the people of Tadmur have narrow, nearly-closed eyes?"

"My son, you have asked a great question," Hillel said; then he pondered the answer. "The reason is that this city is in the desert, and the wind blows sand in the eyes of the desert dwellers. Therefore, God in His pity made their eyes narrow so that the sand would not hurt them."

The man left, waited a while, and again returned, shouting as if he didn't know, "Which one here is Hillel? Which one here is Hillel?"

Hillel got dressed for the third time, went out and asked him patiently, "My son, what do you want?"

"I have a question for you!" shouted the man.

"Ask, my son, ask the question," said Hillel kindly.

"Why do the people of Africa have wide feet?" grumbled the man.

This time, too, Hillel answered carefully.

"My son, you have asked a very worthwhile question. The reason is that the people of Africa live in a place which is very muddy and God made their feet wide so that they would not sink into the muddy swamps of the jungle."

The man saw that he could not get Hillel angry, and he thought to himself, "Now I will talk to him arrogantly. I will curse him and then I will be able to collect the money on my bet."

So he said to Hillel, "I have many questions to ask you, but I am afraid that you will become angry at me."

Hillel invited the man to sit down. He spoke calmly, without rushing him.

"Ask all the questions you want. I will try to answer them."

"Are you the same Hillel who is known as the Nasi of Israel?" the man asked.

"Yes," answered Hillel.

"If you are the one, then I wish that there will not be many like you in Israel!" said the man bitterly.

Without getting angry at all, Hillel asked him calmly, "Why, my son?"

The man replied in anger, "Because of you, I lost four hundred silver coins. My friend promised

*"I have many questions to ask you, but I am
afraid that you will become angry."*

me all this money if I could get you angry, and you didn't lose your patience at all!"

"Be careful not to bet on such things," Hillel replied. "It is better to lose twice four hundred coins than to get Hillel angry."

The man left Hillel. He had learned his lesson and was ashamed of his behavior.

Source: Talmud Bavli, Shabbath, 30-31

Hillel and the heathen

In the days of the Holy Temple, there lived in Jerusalem two great rabbis. One was Shammai and the other was Hillel. Shammai was easily angered when someone did not conduct himself properly. Hillel, on the other hand, was a patient man. He never became angry.

One time, a heathen came to Shammai and said:

"I want to become a Jew. But I make one condition. Teach me the whole Torah while I stand on one foot!"

When Shammai heard this condition, he became angry at the foolish man. Imagine, he wanted to learn the whole Torah while standing on one foot! Why, even a whole lifetime of study will not make a man know the entire Torah!

Shammai took a long measuring stick in his hand, pushed the heathen outside and chased him from the house.

So the heathen went to Hillel.

"I want to become a Jew, but on the condition

"on condition that you teach me the whole Torah while I stand on one foot!"

that you teach me the whole Torah while I stand on one foot!" he demanded.

"Good. I will do as you say," Hillel patiently replied.

The heathen stood on one foot and Hillel taught him, "Whatever is hateful to you, do not do unto your fellow man. This is the whole Torah. Now go and learn all the laws so that you will know what to do and what not to do."

The heathen listened to Hillel's words. He studied the Torah and became a good Jew.

Source: Talmud Bavli, Shabbath, 31

7

The goodness of our Sages

God's blessing
for a good deed

n the city of Antioch there lived a good man who was very generous and very charitable. He gave to the poor and he helped to support the sages who studied the Torah day and night, and did not have the time to work for a living.

The man always gave willingly and graciously. His name was Abba Yudon.

For a time, Abba Yudon prospered. But the good days were soon over. Ill fortune befell him. He lost all of his money, and he was forced to sell his fields in order to buy food for his wife and family. In the end, he had only one field left.

One day, three great sages arrived in the city to collect money for poor scholars. When Abba Yudon saw Rabbi Eliezer, Rabbi Yehoshua and Rabbi Akiva, the three great masters, he was sad and upset, for he remembered that he had always given of his wealth freely to charity, and now he had nothing.

Abba Yudon came home looking very distressed. His wife was frightened by his sad appearance. "What has befallen you?" she asked. "Are you sick, God forbid? Why do you look so haggard?"

Abba Yudon replied sadly, "Our masters have come to town to collect money for charity. We have nothing to give."

The wife of Abba Yudon was even more righteous than her husband. She pondered for a while and said, "We still have one field left. Go and sell half of it, and give the money to the sages."

Abba Yudon was pleased with her advice. He went immediately and sold half the field, and he gave the scholars the money which he received in exchange.

In their great wisdom, our sages understood all that Abba Yudon had done. They saw his righteousness by his acts of charity.

What did they do? They recorded his contribution at the head of the list, even though others had given more than he, and they prayed to God that He help Abba Yudon and bless him in return for his good deeds. The rabbis blessed him, saying, "May the Lord fill all your needs. May it be His will that all you have given to charity be returned to you." Then they went and distributed the money to the poor and needy.

One day, Abba Yudon went to plow the part of the field which still belonged to him. His cow, the only one he had left, was pulling the plow. Suddenly, a pit appeared under her and she fell into the hole and broke her leg.

What a misfortune for Abba Yudon! How would he plow his field now that his cow was hurt? But Abba Yudon did not complain and did not despair over the misfortunes which befell him. Instead he went down quietly to the pit to help his poor cow. Inside the pit he saw something sparkling and shiny. He looked more closely, and to his amazement, a great treasure was lying at the bottom of the pit.

Abba Yudon was happy, and he thanked God saying:

"The Holy One, blessed be He, does everything for the best. My cow broke her foot so that I would find this treasure. It was all done for my good."

From now on, Abba Yudon would have no more worries. With the new-found gold, he bought his fields back and his beautiful home. He also purchased cows, goats and lambs, camels and oxen and other things he needed.

After a time, the rabbis came back to the city, and they asked the people about Abba Yudon. The people said, "Abba Yudon? Are you referring to the man who has many servants? The one who has houses and fields, cows and camels, goats and sheep? He is a very wealthy and important man!"

Abba Yudon heard about the rabbis' arrival and he went to greet them and invite them to his

"My cow broke her foot so that I would find this treasure."

home. The sages asked him, "What are you doing these days, Abba Yudon? How are you?"

Abba Yudon replied, "The Holy One, blessed be He, answered your prayers on my behalf. He has given me many blessings." Then he proceeded to tell them about all that had happened to him.

The rabbis then honored him with their company, and rejoiced with him over the blessings God sent him. Abba Yudon was amply rewarded for his charitable deeds, for even in time of need he had remembered the poor.

Source: Midrash Vayikra Rabbah, chapter 5

The pious man rescues the sick

bba Tachna was a pious man who loved God and observed the commandments of the Torah. During the week he worked outside of the city, and only on the eve of the Sabbath he came home, bringing with him a bundle full of food and clothes for his family.

In spite of the heavy load, Abba Tachna walked briskly in order to be home in time for the Sabbath.

As he walked, Abba Tachna was busy with his thoughts. "How happy my wife and children will be with all the good things I am bringing them! They are, no doubt, very hungry by now, those poor dears."

Abba Tachna quickened his pace and came steadily closer to the city which was his home.

He was on the road leading to the city when a strange sight made him stop suddenly. There, lying in the middle of the road, was a man crying and groaning. Abba Tachna came closer to see what had happened. He saw that the man was covered with bruises from head to toe. The man was so hurt that he couldn't move.

The sick man begged Abba Tachna, "Please help me, rabbi. Have pity on me and take me to the city. I am too sick to move. If I remain here alone, I will die of pain and hunger."

Abba Tachna thought: "What shall I do? I haven't enough strength to carry both the man and the bundle. If I bring the sick man home, my bundle might be stolen and I might not be able to get home in time for the Sabbath. And then, how will my family live without the supplies I am bringing home? Except for my bundle, I have nothing. But if I bring the bundle home first, and then come for the sick man, he might die, God forbid."

Abba Tachna did not think long. The decision was clear.

"First, I will see to it that the man gets home," he decided, "and then I will worry about my bundle."

He put down the bundle, loaded the man onto his shoulders, and walked slowly and carefully so as not to hurt him. With much trouble, he finally reached the sick man's house and put him to bed. Then he hurried back to the road to pick up his bundle. Fortunately, the bundle was in the same place in which he had left it.

Abba Tachna picked up his load and hurried

home towards the city. In the meantime, it was getting late and the sun was setting when he entered. All the townspeople were walking to the synagogue, dressed in their Sabbath clothes, carrying their prayer books. And there was Abba Tachna, still in his working clothes, with a big bundle on his shoulders.

The townspeople were very surprised and said to one another, "Could this be the pious Abba Tachna who is so careful about observing the commandments? Look, now we see him desecrating the Sabbath!"

Abba Tachna himself was worried. "Perhaps I really have desecrated the Sabbath, God forbid," he thought.

The Holy One, blessed be He, saw how troubled this man was, and he returned the sun to the heavens. People saw the sun shining brightly, and they knew the Sabbath had not yet begun.

Abba Tachna hurried home, bathed, got dressed in honor of the Sabbath, and went to the synagogue. He, too, was happy that the Lord came to his aid and gave him the opportunity to do two mitzvoth — to rescue a sick man and to get his bundle of supplies for his family without desecrating the Sabbath.

Source: Midrash Koheleth Rabbah, chapter 9

The guardian
of a treasure

A poor laborer once worked for a land-owner. Every day he would go out to plow the fields and do all the farm chores that needed to be done. With the wages he received, he would buy food for his family. Although he worked long and hard, his earnings were hardly sufficient to buy enough bread. But the man did not complain and was always happy with his lot.

One day, as he was hard at work in the field, Elijah the Prophet appeared to him dressed as an Arab. He greeted the laborer, and the laborer returned his greeting. Then Elijah said, "The Lord knows that you are a poor, hard-working man. He wants to give you six years of riches and with your new wealth you will be able to buy anything you desire. When do you want those six years of plenty — now or later?" asked Elijah.

The laborer did not know that the man in Arab clothing was Elijah the Prophet, and therefore he did not believe the stranger's promises of wealth. So he replied, "Please do not disturb me. I have

133 🌷

work to do in order to earn money for food and clothing for my wife and little children. I have no presents to give you, so go in peace!"

Elijah the Prophet went away, but the next day he came back again and spoke to the poor man as he was plowing the fields. "God wants to give you six years in which you will have riches and comfort. When do you want those years to come?"

The poor man was annoyed at being disturbed from his work, and he said impatiently, "Go in peace. Don't delay me. I do not believe your words."

But when Elijah the Prophet returned for a third time the following day, the laborer realized that perhaps the stranger was telling the truth. So he said, "Wait here please, and I will go and ask my wife."

The laborer came home and told his wife the story of the stranger and the treasure.

"For the past three days, a man dressed as an Arab has been coming to me, and he has told me that God wants to give me six years of wealth. He wants to know whether I want the good years now or later. What shall I tell him?"

His wife replied, "Ask for God to send you the good fortune at once!"

The man returned to the field and found Elijah the Prophet waiting for him. He said to him, "We would like to have the good years now rather than later."

"Good," said Elijah the Prophet with satisfaction. "Go back home and you will find that the Lord has blessed you."

The poor man returned home. Meanwhile, his children were playing in the sand when they found a box full of money. "Come, Mother, and see what we have found!" they called in excitement.

The mother saw that there was enough money in the box to live comfortably for some years. When the father got home and his family told him about the new-found treasure, he was very happy and he praised God for His goodness. Then he turned back to his wife. "How shall we spend this money?" he asked.

His wife answered wisely, "We will not buy unnecessary things, nor will we eat delicacies. We will use the money only for food and the clothes we really need. The rest we will keep for charity and to do good works."

The woman sent her son to buy a notebook and a pen. Every day she told him, "Mark the amount that we gave to charity." The boy did as his mother told him. So they cared for the sick, fed the hungry, and bought warm clothes for poor children.

After six years, Elijah the Prophet returned to

the man and said to him, "The time has come for you to return everything God has given you."

"Before I give up my wealth," said the laborer, "I will go home and let my wife know."

"The old man has come to take back the money," he told his wife.

His wife replied, "Show Elijah our journal in which we have kept a record of the money and how we have spent it. Tell him, 'If there are people who use the money for better purposes than we do, then entrust the money to those who use it well.' "

And God was aware of all the good they had done with the money which He had sent them. Therefore, He ordered Elijah the Prophet not to take away their wealth. On the contrary! He told him to increase their fortunes, so that they could live in peace and do good deeds all their lives.

Source: Midrash Yalkut Shimoni, 427

Hillel's wife
and the poor man

illel was so poor in his early days
that he didn't even have enough
bread to eat. Only later, when he
became the Nasi, the prince, in
Israel was he well-to-do. But even then he lived
simply, and his wife used to prepare the meals
herself.

An important guest once came to the old and
respected Hillel. Hillel wanted to treat his visitor
to a delicious meal, so he went to his wife and said,
"Please prepare a tasty meal for our guest."

Hillel's wife hurried to the kitchen and kneaded some dough to bake bread, for in those days
there were no bakeries and every woman baked her
own bread. She lit the oven and put in the dough.
Then she prepared meat with vegetables and
relishes. Finally everything was finished and
tastefully prepared.

The wife was about to bring the bread and the
other food to Hillel and his guest, when she heard a
knock at the door. She opened the door, and there

was a young man standing in the doorway, sad and forlorn.

"Welcome. May I help you?" she asked.

The man answered, "Today is my wedding day. The bride and the wedding guests are assembled and waiting. But I have not earned any money for a long time, and my bride is poor, too. We do not have the means to prepare the feast for the wedding guests, and I am ashamed to come to the ceremony empty-handed."

The wife of Hillel took the bread and all the tasty delicacies that she had prepared for their guest, and gave them to the man. The poor man gratefully took the food. He carried the meal to the guests who had come to attend his wedding, and they enjoyed a festive dinner.

And then what did Hillel's wife do?

She started all the preparations anew. She kneaded and baked bread again, and she cooked the other food.

All this time, Hillel sat with his visitor and they studied the words of Torah together. It was late and the visitor was hungry. Hillel was very surprised that his wife had not yet brought the meal, but he did not want to call her. He knew that his wife was a good woman, and her intentions were good no matter what she did.

At last she came in. She set the table and brought in the meal.

The wife of Hillel took the bread and all the tasty
delicacies and gave them to the man

"Why didn't you serve us right away, my dear?" Hillel asked her.

His wife told him the story. "A poor man came to the house and said that this was the day of his wedding, and he had no food to serve the wedding guests. So I gave him all the food I had and I prepared the meal all over again."

Hearing this, Hillel praised her and said, "My dear, you did all these things for the sake of Heaven. God will surely be pleased with your deeds of kindness."

Source: Talmud Bavli, Derech Eretz, chapter 6

The secret gift

There was a great rabbi in Babylonia and his name was Mar Ukva. He studied the Torah all day, and he was occupied with good deeds in much of the time left. He gave many gifts to the poor. In order not to embarrass them, Mar Ukva did not send the money through others, but he went quietly and distributed the gifts himself.

"If the poor do not know who their benefactor is," thought the righteous Mar Ukva, "they will give thanks to God alone." For this reason, he did not give them the money directly. Instead, he silently came near the house of the poor man, threw the money through a crack in the door, and quickly went off. The poor man would find the money, but not the person who had put it there.

Every day Mar Ukva left gifts for the poor in this way.

It happened once that Mar Ukva remained in the House of Study later than usual. His wife came to see how he was and why he was late coming home.

The goodness of our Sages

Mar Ukva had not yet had a chance to give out the charity that day. So after he finished his studies, he took his wife along with him on his errand of kindness.

The poor man for whom the money was being left remained at home that day. He had become curious and said to himself, "I will stay here until I see the wonderful stranger who leaves charity at my door every day. I want to find out who the kind man is."

Mar Ukva and his wife were coming closer and were turning into the entrance of his house. At that moment the poor man looked outside.

"Certainly these are the people who have been leaving money for me!" he exclaimed, and rushed to thank them for their kindness.

But when Mar Ukva and his wife caught sight of him, they ran away as fast as they could because they did not want to embarrass the man. They looked for a place to hide, and they stumbled upon a big bakery oven. The oven fire was out, so they felt safe enough to hide in it. But alas, what trouble! The floor of the oven was still very hot and Mar Ukva's feet were painfully burned by the hot bricks.

His wife was alarmed. "Put your feet on mine," she said, "because my feet are not hurt."

Why was the good wife spared the burns and the pain? Because she always gave food to the

"Put your feet on mine; my feet are not hurt."

poor, and that was even better than giving money to them. So the Holy One, blessed be He, performed a miracle for her as a reward for her kindness, and she was unharmed by the hot oven.

Mar Ukva and his wife waited until the poor man gave up looking for them. Then they quickly deposited the money and returned home.

Why did they enter a hot oven and risk being burned?

They did not want to embarrass the poor man for taking charity from other people. Rather, they wanted to show the poor man that the Holy One, blessed be He, sent the money through an unknown messenger, for the help comes from the Lord, and it is not important to know through which messenger God sends His help.

Source: Talmud Bavli, Kethuvoth 67b

Giving help honorably

nce there was a lonely little boy who had no one in the world, no mother and no father, no aunt or uncle, and no other relatives.

The boy wandered aimlessly through the streets, hungry and sad. A kind man found him and took him home. He fed the boy and gave him good clothes to wear and a clean bed in which to sleep.

The boy stayed with the man and made his home with him. He went to school and studied for a time. When he grew up to be a young man, he learned a trade, so that he would be able to earn his food by himself.

In addition the good man set him up with a house, and gave him money to open a workshop. In a short time, the young man became very prosperous.

But the man who had been so kind to the boy had sudden reverses of fortune. He lost his possessions and became very poor.

"I will go to the young man of whom I took care all these years, and I will ask him for a gift of money to tide me over," said the man. "He will surely want to help me."

The kind man did as he planned. He called on the young man and was welcomed warmly. The two of them chatted in affection and friendship. They spoke at length of many things. The impoverished man was ashamed to ask for a handout, but at last he summoned enough courage to say in a meek and humble voice: "I have come to ask a favor — a loan. I have lost all of my fortunes and I have almost nothing left."

The young man was very sad, because the person who had dealt so kindly with him and had given so much to the poor, must now himself ask for donations.

He comforted his friend. And to himself, he thought, "I wonder how I can help this good man without embarrassing him." Then he had an idea. "I will give him a nice present without letting him know that he received it from me." At the same time, he told the man, "The Lord will make you as prosperous as before."

He did not give the poor man a loan directly, excusing himself in this way: "It is hard for me to give you money now. I don't have any at the moment. But I will see . . . I will try . . . we will talk some more about this matter."

The man took leave of his friend and went home.

As soon as he left, the young man called one of his servants and instructed him to put on patched and torn clothes. Then he gave him a precious pearl and sent him to the home of the good man. When the man answered the door, the servant showed him the precious jewel.

"Do you want to buy a beautiful pearl cheaply?" he asked.

"How much is it?" the man asked.

"One coin," the servant replied.

"That is very cheap!" thought the man. "I have one coin left. But I guess it will be worth spending it for this purchase. I should be able to sell the pearl at a profit." So he bought the pearl and paid for it with his only silver coin.

After a few days, the young man sent another one of his servants who, unlike the first one, was dressed in beautiful clothes. The master gave him a great deal of money and told him just what to do. The servant, dressed as a rich man, went to the home of the good man and said, "I have heard that one can buy pearls from you. I would like very much to have a beautiful pearl. Perhaps you have one for sale?"

The man brought out the pearl which he had bought just a few days before for one silver coin, and showed it to the customer.

147

"Do you want to buy a beautiful pearl cheaply?"

"Exactly the kind I want," the servant said. "Will you sell it for a thousand silver coins?"

The man readily agreed to sell the jewel, and the servant returned the jewel to his master.

The poor man thus received a large sum of money, not knowing at all that it was really a gift from the young man. Happily he went to the young man and said, "You need not try to help me any more. Thank God, I was able to make a good sale, and I was left with a fine profit."

And so both were pleased. The good man was happy not to have to ask for a donation, and the young man was happy to be able to give charity without embarrassing the one who received it.

Source: Me'il Tzedakah

They watched
what they said

Speaking good and evil

Rabban Shimon ben Gamliel was one of the presidents of the Sanhedrin, the rabbinic court in Israel. He was the grandson of Hillel and, like his grandfather, he was a man of great wisdom and a scholar of the Holy Torah.

Many people learned from him and grew wise. Among them was Tovi, his servant, who was always in his master's company in order to serve him.

One day Rabbi Shimon called Tovi and said to him: "Please go to the market and buy some delicious, tasty food."

Tovi went to the butcher and bought the tongue of a cow and gave it to Rabbi Shimon. "Here," he said, "I have brought you a delicacy."

"Fine!" said Rabbi Shimon. "And now go and buy me something bad to eat."

Tovi was puzzled, but he kept quiet, and he went back to the market as his master had ordered. On the way to the market he thought: "Why did Rabbi Shimon tell me to buy bad food

for him? Why does he need this kind of food? He surely wants to teach me and his students an important lesson. But I wonder what the lesson could be?"

Tovi thought for a while, and suddenly he understood!

When he got to the market, he went into the butcher shop again. And what do you think he bought? Another tongue!

He returned to his master with the second tongue which he had just purchased.

"Tell me, Tovi," asked Rabbi Shimon, "why have you done this? When I asked you to buy me a tasty delicacy, you bought me a tongue. Now that I have asked you to buy me bad food, you got a tongue again. Is the tongue both good and bad?"

"In reality it is just that," answered Tovi. "When the tongue is good there is nothing better, and when it is bad there is nothing worse. When people speak the words of the Torah and recite the prayers," continued Tovi, "and when they speak kind and wise words to each other, the tongue is very good. But if people speak harshly and with insult to upset others, the tongue is very bad."

Rabbi Shimon ben Gamliel was happy that Tovi, his servant, understood well the lesson he was to learn in the marketplace. He hastened to explain the story to his students so that they, too, would guard their tongues against speaking evil.

"When the tongue is good there is nothing better,
and when it is bad there is nothing worse."

They watched what they said

From Tovi they would learn that it is well to speak gently and kindly to each other always.

Source: Midrash Vayikra Rabbah, chapter 33

Soft tongues
and hard tongues

abbi, the son of Rabbi Shimon ben Gamliel, also wanted his pupils to remember to speak gently and carefully to their fellow-men.

What did he do?

He invited all his pupils to a feast and ordered two kinds of food. He asked to be served well-cooked tongues which were soft and tender, and partly cooked tongues which were half-raw and tough.

Rabbi himself came to the feast. "Please eat, my sons," he said to his pupils. "Choose any of the tongues you want."

Not one of his students wanted to eat the hard tongues. They all chose to eat the tasty tender ones.

Rabbi observed this and said with satisfaction: "Look carefully, my sons, so that you may understand what you are doing. All of you have left the hard tongues and chosen the soft ones instead."

Then he continued. "I hope you will behave this way in speaking to each other. Don't speak

They watched what they said

with a harsh and angry tone, but use a soft tongue to speak gently and kindly to one another."

Source: Midrash Vayikra Rabbah, chapter 33

 158

The best medicine

ot far from the city of Zippori there lived a salesman who used to sell medicines and spices of all kinds. Every day he went with his merchandise from city to city and from street to street. He came to the marketplace and to the courtyards and called in a loud voice: "Whoever wants to live long, come buy this potion of life! Whoever wants a wonderful medicine, come to me!"

Everywhere, people hearing the chant, peeked out the windows and came running to the salesman. For who would not want to buy a wonderful cure that promises long life?

In one of the cities the salesman visited there lived a teacher named Rabbi Yannai. Rabbi Yannai was at home studying the Torah, when suddenly he heard a voice outside announcing: "Come and buy a wonderful cure — a medicine for long life!"

Rabbi Yannai looked out the window to the street, and he saw the salesman surrounded by many customers.

159 🌺

"Come and buy a wonderful cure —
a medicine for long life."

"What is this medicine the man is prescribing for people?" thought Rabbi Yannai. "I must find out if he is telling the truth!"

He called to the salesman at once.

"Hear, my good man," he said, "Please come up and sell me your wonderful medicine."

When the salesman saw the rabbi, he was embarrassed. "Rabbi," he said, "you and people like you, who study the Torah all day and fulfill the commandments of God, don't need this medicine."

"Just the same, please come up and show me," said Rabbi Yannai.

The salesman did not want to come at first, but Rabbi Yannai urged him and persisted until he finally agreed to go to the house of the rabbi.

"Now," said Rabbi Yannai, "where is the miracle cure?"

The salesman opened his bag and took out a Book of Psalms. In it are written the songs and prayers of King David, may he rest in peace. The salesman gave the book to the rabbi.

"Is this the medicine for long life?" asked the rabbi.

The salesman opened the book and pointed to the sentence: "Who is the man who wants life — guard your tongue from speaking evil." Then he said, "I teach this sentence to all the people who come to buy anything."

161

They watched what they said

"You are right," said Rabbi Yannai, "so this is the potion of life! Only now do I fully understand this beautiful sentence. King David cautioned us to keep our tongue from saying unkind things about other people. If we will do so, the Lord will grant us long life in the Garden of Eden, in paradise. Also, King Solomon, who was the wisest of all men, said, 'One who guards his mouth and tongue, guards his soul from trouble!' That is really a wonderful medicine. May many people buy it. Go in peace, my good man!"

Source: Midrash Vayikra Rabbah, chapter 16

A love of Torah
and those who learn it

Studying Torah
in poverty

Before Hillel became the Nasi, the Prince in Israel, he was very poor. Nevertheless, as long as he had enough money to feed his wife and children, and as long as he could pay the doorman at the house of study to enter and to study the Torah from the great teachers — Shemaya and Avtalyon — he was very happy.

Hillel worked hard but earned very little. He used one half of his earnings to buy bread for himself and his family, and the rest of the money he gave to the doorkeeper at the house of study.

Every day Hillel divided his earnings between his family and his school. He was thankful to be able to study the Torah.

But one day he could not find work and he didn't earn anything. That was on a Friday, the day before the Sabbath. He was sad that he did not have any money to buy Sabbath candles, wine for Kiddush, flour for challah, but he was most upset because he could not get into the house of study. So he stood outside and looked into the school.

"There inside are my rabbis with their pupils sitting in front of them, learning the words of the Torah," Hillel thought, "and here I am outside unable to enter. I wish I could hear their words!"

This was in the month of Teveth, in the middle of winter, and it was very cold outside.

Inside, in the house of study, it was warm and pleasant. But Hillel was not longing for the warmth of the oven. He longed for the warmth of Torah! And then he remembered that on the roof there was an opening, a window to let in light and air. He should be able to hear from there! He quickly climbed up on the roof without letting the watchman see. He bent over, and through the opening in the roof he heard the words of Torah from Shemaya and Avtalyon. He was even able to see the teachers as they were were sitting near the warm oven. The entire day Hillel lay on the roof listening. He did not feel the cold at all — so great was his love of Torah.

But night came and it was freezing outside. Hillel was stiff from the cold. He lay down near the chimney to keep warm, for he had no strength to get up.

In the meantime, snow started falling, slowly covering him from head to toe. He did not feel anything, because he fainted from weakness.

166

*Through the opening in the roof he heard the
words of Torah of Shemaya and Avtalyon*

In the house of study, the people welcomed the Sabbath, prayed and went home, made Kiddush on the wine and ate the Sabbath meal. After that they returned and continued studying all night. They loved the Torah so much that they did not want to interrupt their studies even for sleep. So they sat there studying until morning.

At the break of dawn, when it was beginning to get light outside, Shemaya said to Avtalyon, "Avtalyon, my brother, why isn't there any daylight in this room? It is morning already, and it is still dark inside. Perhaps it is a cloudy day, and the sun is not visible at all."

They glanced up towards the roof window to look for thick clouds in the sky, and behold, what did they see there? The form of a man stretched out on the roof!

All the people in the house of study were alarmed. The students went up on the roof at once. They dug in the snow until they uncovered the person lying there. They looked at him, and behold, it was their friend Hillel!

The pupils quickly brought him down to the house of study. They washed him and rubbed him with snow so that he would wake up. Even though it was the Sabbath, they washed him and rubbed him with oil. Then they sat him in front of the fire until he was warmed and revived.

Shemaya and Avtalyon taught, "A Jew is

permitted to desecrate the Sabbath in order to save a person's life. This man Hillel, who endangered his life in order to study Torah, is certainly deserving of having the Sabbath desecrated on his account."

Hillel recovered and he continued to study with his teachers every day. In time he became a very wise man, a teacher and a leader for all of Israel.

Source: Talmud Bavli, Yoma 35

Wealth and Torah

here was a man in Israel whose name was Charsom. He was a man of great wealth. He owned a thousand cities and all the houses in them. The people who lived in the cities were obligated to work for him.

He had a fleet of ships at sea that sailed to faraway places. They brought back whatever he desired — gold and precious stones, fragrant spices and fine silk for clothing. Charsom would sell the merchandise that the ships brought from those distant places. The trading made him richer and richer.

Charsom had only one son named Elazar. When the father grew old and died, Elazar, his only son, inherited all his wealth, including the cities and the ships.

Elazar did not like all the wealth his father had left him. He had no desire to see the cities he owned or any of his ships that sailed the seas to bring back precious cargo.

Elazar loved the Holy Torah more than

anything and his only wish was to be left alone to study the Torah without interruption.

But merchants who came to buy and sell were always interrupting him. Servants were constantly calling to ask what he wished to eat and drink. All sorts of people came regularly to honor him as they would honor any man of great wealth.

To escape all this, Elazar put on the simple clothes of a poor man. He took a sack full of flour on his shoulders, so that he could bake bread when he got hungry, and he quietly went out of the house. He walked a long time until he made his way to another city, there to study the Torah.

He did not remain long in this city either, because he was afraid that people would recognize him. For fear of being disturbed from his studies, he moved to still another city. And so he wandered from city to city, and from state to state. In every city he sought out the rabbi or the yeshiva (a school for the study of Torah), where he settled among the students to study with great diligence and much joy.

After a few years, he became a rabbi himself and he was known as Rabbi Elazar ben Charsom. Even after he became rabbi, he continued to go from place to place to increase his knowledge of the Torah.

Once while he was walking along the way, he chanced to meet some of his servants. They did not

171

recognize him, for he appeared to be poor. His clothes were simple and shabby, and he had a sack of food on his back. His servants called to him. "Stop! Why are you walking about here, idle and not working?" they asked. "We saw you leaving the city which belongs to our master Rabbi Elazar ben Charsom. You are our master's servant, and so you must go to work for him. Come back with us at once and we will give you work to do!"

Rabbi Elazar did not want to tell them that he was the master, and so he said to them, "Please let me continue on my way, for I want to be left in peace to study the Torah."

"You lazy good-for-nothing!" shouted the servants. "We will not let go of you! You must go to work for Rabbi Elazar, our master!"

Rabbi Elazar pleaded with them to set him free, but they refused to listen. He absolutely did not want to tell them who he was. So he took money which he had brought along for traveling expenses and he gave it to them. "Please take my money and let me go," he said.

The servants took the money and went away. Rabbi Elazar continued his journey very happily, for money was not at all important to him. His only desire was to be allowed to spend all his time in the study of Torah without interruption.

Source: Talmud Bavli, Yoma 35

"Please take my money and let me go."

Eliezer ben Hyrcanus

abbi Eliezer ben Hyrcanus was one of the greatest and most important of our scholars, may their memory be for a blessing. But when he was young, he did not study the Torah at all. He did not even know the prayers, or the recitation of the Shema, or Grace After Meals. He was a large and sturdy young man. He worked the soil and every day he would go out with his brothers to plow his father's fields.

His brothers worked in the valley where the soil was even and loose. Eliezer plowed on the hill, where the soil was hard and rocky. One day he sat in the field crying. His father came over, "Why are you crying?" he asked in alarm. "Is it because your brothers have easy work and you have to plow this rocky soil? Don't cry! You may now plow with your brothers in the valley where it is easier," his father reassured him.

Eliezer went down to plow in the valley, but he was still in tears. His father was curious. "Why are you crying now?" he wanted to know. "Are you sorry that I sent you to this valley to plow?"

"No," answered Eliezer.

"Why are you crying, then? What is the matter?" asked his father.

"Because I want to study Torah," replied Eliezer. "If I have enough strength to plow soil full of rocks, I would have enough strength to study the Torah, too."

His father laughed. "You want to study the Torah! A fellow as big as you will now start to study?" he said. "You are old enough to marry. When you have children of your own, you will take *them* to school to study!"

But Eliezer was not convinced. "I will go to Jerusalem, and I will study with the great teacher Rabbi Yochanan ben Zakkai," he said.

His father was angry at him now. "You must plow the whole field! You will not get anything to eat until you finish!" he shouted.

Hyrcanus thought: "My son will work hard and he will forget that he wanted to study Torah."

Eliezer rose early the following morning. When his work in the field was finished, he did not return home for the meal as was his custom. He had made his decision and he didn't waste a minute. He started out on foot for Jerusalem. He took no supplies with him, and he had no money to buy food. When he became very hungry, he took a mouthful of soil and chewed it so that he wouldn't feel his hunger.

At last he came to Jerusalem and went to the house of study where Rabbi ben Zakkai was teaching. Eliezer sat quietly on the side. He listened carefully but could not understand a word, for he had never, until now, studied anything. So he sat quietly with tears in his eyes.

Rabbi Yochanan saw the strange young man crying. "Why are you so upset, my son?" asked the Rabbi.

"Because I wish to study and understand the Torah, as your other students do," answered Eliezer.

Rabbi Yochanan looked at him and observed that he was a grown lad and not a child just starting to study.

"Haven't you learned anything until now?" he asked.

"Nothing," answered Eliezer.

"If that is so," said Rabbi Yochanan, "I will now teach you the most simple prayers, the recitation of the Shema and Grace After Meals."

Rabbi Yochanan began to teach him. Eliezer was a good student. He repeated everything until he knew it well. Rabbi Yochanan ben Zakkai taught him more and more, and Eliezer went over his studies many times until he mastered the new work.

In the meantime, Eliezer had no food to eat and went hungry all the time. He loved the study of the Torah so much that he forgot about eating. Eight days passed. Rabbi Yochanan ben Zakkai, his teacher, sensed a strange odor coming from his pupil's mouth. It was the smell of hunger and chewing on dust.

Rabbi Yochanan realized that Eliezer, his diligent pupil, probably had not eaten for a long time. So he called him over.

"Eliezer, have you eaten today?" asked the teacher. Eliezer was ashamed to tell him that he had not had a meal for eight days, so he remained silent.

Rabbi Yochanan ben Zakkai whispered to two of his students to go to the lodging where Eliezer was staying and find out if he had any meals there. The students came to the house where Eliezer was staying, and they asked the lady of the house: "Does our friend Eliezer live here?"

"Yes, yes," answered the woman.

"Has Eliezer been taking his meals with you?" they asked.

"No," she said. Then she added, "We thought that he is eating at the home of Rabbi Yochanan ben Zakkai. But I saw him take out something

177

from his bag and chew on it. Perhaps he has food in the sack."

They opened the bag and they saw that there was no food, just dust of the earth!

The students went back to Rabbi Yochanan and told him the story. Rabbi Yochanan immediately called Eliezer.

"Eliezer, my son," he said. "Just as you had a strange odor because you had not eaten for eight days, so you will have a great name among all people. You will be a wise and distinguished man some day!"

Rabbi Yochanan paused, and added, "From this day forward you will always eat at my table."

Eliezer stayed with Rabbi Yochanan ben Zakkai and studied Torah day and night. Many years passed in study, until he became a very learned man.

One day, Rabbi Yochanan made a feast and invited all the wise men of Israel and the important and respected people in Jerusalem. They sat together at the table and Rabbi Yochanan was leading a Torah discussion.

Suddenly a stranger appeared among the guests, a man who had not been invited. He was Abba Hyrcanus, the father of Rabbi Eliezer!

Hyrcanus did not come to take part in the feast. Rather, he came to complain about his son

Eliezer, who had left him in his old age and had run away to Jerusalem.

When he arrived in Jerusalem and inquired about the whereabouts of Rabbi Yochanan ben Zakkai, he was told by the townspeople: "You can find him at a feast in his home today."

This is how Hyrcanus came to the feast.

Rabbi Yochanan recognized Hyrcanus as the father of his disciple, Rabbi Eliezer.

"Make room for him among the honored guests here," he ordered his students.

Hyrcanus was seated in a prominent place at the head of the table. He was trembling in surprise. "Why are they giving me so much honor?" he wondered.

Now Hyrcanus saw that Rabbi Yochanan called on one of his students to get up and lecture on the Torah before all the guests. Who do you think the student was? Eliezer, his son, of course!

Rabbi Eliezer arose and spoke words of Torah, beautiful and eloquent, as pleasing to the listeners as the words of the Torah were to the children of Israel at the time of the receiving of the Torah on Mt. Sinai.

Rabbi Yochanan ben Zakkai got up from his seat and kissed Rabbi Eliezer on his head with love and happiness.

Hyrcanus, Eliezer's father, was overcome with

179 🌹

joy and pride. He arose and spoke to all the guests.

"My teachers and rabbis! I have come to Jerusalem to complain about Eliezer. I wanted to punish my son by not granting him any of my treasures! But now that I have seen what a great scholar he is, I have changed my mind. All my possessions are his. He will even get his brothers' shares."

"Father," answered Rabbi Eliezer. "If I had wanted gold and silver, I could have asked the Holy One, blessed be He, and He would have granted me riches. But I did not come here to seek honor or money. I came here because I love the Torah. Give your treasures to my brothers. I do not deserve any more than they. I ask nothing from the Holy One, blessed be He, only to be able to study Torah."

Rabbi Eliezer remained in Jerusalem and studied Torah until he became the teacher of all Israel.

Sources: Midrash Bereshith Rabbah, chapter 42
    Avoth de Rabbi Nathan, chapter 6
    Pirkey de Rabbi Eliezer

Hyrcanus was overcome with joy and pride

The wise man
and the merchants

nce a ship was sailing on the high seas, carrying many passengers to a faraway land. The passengers were taking various goods to the distant land to sell to the people there.

One man had a big bundle of cloth for clothing. Another man had beautiful fruit from the Land of Israel — almonds, raisins, and figs. A third had precious dishes — bowls and pitchers made of gold and stained glass. A fourth man had carpets. A fifth had jewelry — rings, bracelets and necklaces. As for the rest of the passengers — each of them had valuable merchandise with him.

Sitting on the deck, the passengers talked among themselves.

"I have the best merchandise of all. I will earn more profit from my sales than any of you!" each one boasted. Everyone showed his friends the bags and the crates, the bundles and the boxes that he was bringing with him.

There was one man on the ship who did not boast about his merchandise. He did not take part

*One man had a bundle of clothing; another had
beautiful fruit from the Land of Israel*

in the conversation at all. The man had a book in his hand, and he read and studied, without paying attention to anything going on around him.

At first, the passengers left him on his own and did not disturb him. But it was a long journey, and after each man had already told all the stories he had to tell, people became bored. Finally, one passenger turned to the man studying and asked him, "Where is your merchandise? What do you have to sell? How many chests and bundles have you brought with you on the boat?"

The man was not one of the merchants. He was a rabbi and a learned man. He thought for a while, then slowly found an answer.

"My merchandise is more important than yours," he said, "but I have hidden it and you will not be able to find it."

"Why won't you show us your merchandise?" asked the passengers. "Everyone of us has displayed his goods; now you can show us yours."

"Not now. There will come a time when you will see it," the wise man replied.

The merchants searched and scoured every corner of the boat, but they couldn't find even one box or bundle belonging to the scholar. So they laughed at the learned rabbi and said, "You don't have anything. You are showing off in vain!"

The wise man took their jeers in good humor and did not say anything.

Time passed. One day a pirate ship appeared suddenly on the high seas, and came near their boat. In an instant the pirates swooped down upon the merchant ship and stole all the precious cargo — the rugs and vessels, the jewels and cloth, the fruit and all the other valuables. They took everything and fled.

When the ship reached the distant land at last, the merchants had nothing to sell. They did not have any money to buy food. They stood on the street helpless, not knowing what to do or where to turn.

The wise rabbi, on the other hand, went straight to the synagogue. He said his prayers and sat down to study Torah. The Jews of the synagogue saw that the rabbi had come from a faraway land, so they came over and greeted him in a friendly manner. They asked him about many things and he answered all questions sensibly and correctly, for he was very wise and very learned in the Torah.

The people saw his wisdom and they gave him the honor and respect he deserved. They invited him to their homes and asked him to dine with them. They gave him many gifts and asked him to remain with them to become the rabbi in their city. They promised to give him a house and everything he needed.

The rabbi agreed to settle there. All the people

of the city escorted him in a procession to his new house. They walked respectfully on his right and on his left as if he were a king.

In the meantime, the merchants who had come with him on the ship were still standing about in the streets. They were hungry and miserable, but no one even inquired about their sad state of affairs.

When they saw the rabbi, they came over and pleaded: "Please help us, rabbi. You remember that we were rich and that we had many beautiful things to sell, until the pirates came and robbed us of everything. Please tell the people of the city that you know us. Ask them to give us some bread, for we are very hungry and we have nothing left."

The rabbi smiled and said, "You see that my merchandise is better than yours. The Torah which I studied and which I hid in my head is the best possession I have. No robber could have taken it from me. It is because of my Torah learning that I am shown all this honor and respect in this city."

The rabbi looked at the shabby group of merchants and added, "Don't be sad. I will ask the people of this city to help you also."

On hearing the rabbi's plea, the people went and gathered food and clothing. They also gave some money to the penniless merchants so that they could return to their homes.

And the wise rabbi lived in respect and comfort all his days.

Source: Midrash Tanchuma, Trumah

Working and earning food

Pleasure in hard work

n his early years, Rabbi Akiva was very poor. He could barely provide a meager living for his family. Every day he went to the forest, chopped the trees and sawed them into pieces. He bundled the pieces of wood and sold half of them in the marketplace. The money that he earned was spent on food for himself and his wife and children.

And the rest of the chopped wood? That also was very useful to Rabbi Akiva. He put some wood in the oven, kindled a fire, and warmed the house on cold winter days. And he held a burning piece of wood in his hand and by its light he could sit and study the Torah.

He was happiest when he studied. He loved learning so much that he forgot his poverty, and he was always cheerful and contented.

Late at night, when Rabbi Akiva wanted to sleep a little, he spread some of the remaining boards on the floor and he lay down to sleep, for he was so poor that he had no bed. Because he worked very hard and studied very much, he slept soundly even on the hard boards.

Once Rabbi Akiva's neighbors came and complained.

"Akiva, we are bothered by the smoke of the wood which you burn in your house," said the neighbors. "We have a suggestion. Why don't you sell to us the wood that you have left? With the money you earn, buy some oil and a lamp. This way you will get better lighting, and we will not be bothered by the smoke."

The neighbors exaggerated somewhat. In fact, they were not bothered so badly by the smoke, but they thought that by saying so they would make Rabbi Akiva sell them the boards and so they would be able to help him study the Torah in better light. But Rabbi Akiva understood their intention and could not agree to this.

"I cannot sell you the boards," he said. "The wood gives me all that my family and I need — food and warmth, light by which to study Torah, and a bed of boards for rest."

Rabbi Akiva was satisfied with his lot. In the end, God gave him great riches and abundance. So great was his wealth that he dined on tables of gold and silver, and he mounted his bed on ladders of gold.

Source: Avoth de Rabbi Nathan, chapter 6

A man works
not only for himself

ong ago, a Roman king named
Adrianus went out to make war
against his enemies in a distant
land.

On the way the king and his soldiers passed
through the Land of Israel. When he got to a small
village not far from the city of Tiberias, he saw an
old man working in his garden. The man, stooped
with age and years of toil, was bending over and
hoeing the earth. Then he dug holes in the ground
and planted saplings of fig trees. The king stopped
to watch the old man at work.

The old man worked very hard. His hands were
very busy with the saplings and beads of perspi-
ration dripped down his forehead.

The king shook his head in amazement.
"Haven't you worked yet hard enough all your life,
grandfather? How old are you?" he asked.

"I am one hundred years old, Your Majesty,"
replied the old man.

"A man of a hundred standing and bothering to
plant young trees! Why must you work so hard?

"Haven't you worked hard enough all your life, grandfather?"

What good is it to plant these trees? Do you really think that you will live long enough to enjoy the fruit of these trees? You will soon die and others will enjoy the fruits of your labors!" the king said.

"No matter!" answered the old man. "If the Holy One, blessed be He, wills it, I may still live to eat the fruit of the trees that I plant now. And if not, my sons will eat it. Just as my father and grandfather before me planted trees and I later ate the fruit, so will my children enjoy the fruit of my labors."

The king went on his way, together with his soldiers. The war was long and drawn out. It dragged on for three years. When the fighting ended in the fourth year, the king returned the same way he had come and again passed the garden of the old man. Again the king saw the grandfather standing near the fig trees which he had planted. The trees had grown in the meantime and bore sweet and luscious figs.

When the old man saw the king approaching, he hurried and took a little basket, filled it with delicious fruit and presented it to the king.

"Your Majesty," he said, "I am the old man whom you met here more than three years ago when I was planting these figs. The good Lord has made me worthy of staying alive to enjoy the fruit of the trees. Here is my fruit as a gift to your Royal Highness."

195

"I see that God loves you, so I will honor you, too," said the king to the old man.

He turned to his servants and said, "Take the gift from him. Put the figs in another vessel and fill his little basket with gold coins."

The servants did as the king commanded. They took out the figs and filled the basket with gold coins and returned it to the old man.

The grandfather went home happy and contented. He told his wife and children and grandchildren all that had happened. The entire family was indeed proud of the hard-working old grandfather.

Source: Midrash Tanchuma on Kedoshim

The blessings
of hard work

n a foreign land there was a city called Lodkia. At one time the inhabitants of that city needed a great deal of oil — so much that there was not enough oil in the whole city, nor in the entire country, to fill their needs.

The people of the city came together and counseled with each other about the best way to get the oil. They decided that one person among them would go to the Land of Israel to buy it. A wise and faithful messenger was chosen to go on the journey. The people gave him a big purse full of gold coins. "Buy all the oil you can get for this money," they instructed him.

The man started out for Jerusalem and he traveled for many days before he reached his destination. At last he came to the city and met the people of Jerusalem.

"Would you sell me your oil? I will pay you all the money that I have in my purse," he said.

"No," answered the people of Jerusalem. "We don't have very much oil. Go to the city of Tzor.

There you might find what you are looking for."

For many days, the messenger traveled until he reached Tzor. When he arrived he met the inhabitants of that city.

"Won't you sell me some oil?" he asked. "I am ready to pay all the money that I have in my purse."

"No," answered the people of Tzor. "We don't have enough oil to sell you. Go to the city of Gush-Halav. There you might find what you are seeking."

The man took to the road again, and traveled many days until he reached Gush-Halav. "I have come to buy some oil," he told the people. "I am ready to pay all the money that I have in my purse."

The people of Gush-Halav answered: "There is one man in this city who can sell you all the oil you want. Go to the field. You will find him there."

The messenger went to the field, and he came to a grove of olives. There was a man in the grove digging ditches in the ground for planting olive trees.

"Do you have oil for me?" the messenger asked the farmer. "I will pay you all the money I have in my purse. I have traveled a great distance — all the way from the city of Lodkia — for I must buy a large supply of oil for the people of my city."

The man looked at the stranger.

"Do you have oil for me?" the messenger asked.

"Yes, I have enough oil and I can sell you some, but I have not yet finished my work in the fields," said the farmer.

The messenger watched as the man continued his work. When he finished his chores, he put his tools on his shoulders, and the two started for the city.

On the road through the olive orchard the farmer would stop once in a while and bend down to clear the rocks from the soil so the trees would grow better.

The messenger watched the hard-working farmer in surprise.

"A man who has so much oil must be very rich," he thought. "Why does he work so hard, doing everything himself? He even pulls up the rocks in his orchard without any help. But, maybe they were really making fun of me when they told me that I can buy oil for the people of my city from this poor man."

When they came to the farmer's house, his maidservant came running toward him with a kettle full of warm water, so that he could wash his hands and face. Then she brought out a golden basin filled with oil, and the man dipped his hands and feet into it to fulfill the words of Moshe, who had blessed his forefathers from the tribe of Asher, "he will dip his feet in oil" because he will possess it in abundance.

The messenger was now impressed with what he saw, and he realized that this hard-working farmer was truly a man of great wealth.

The man invited the messenger to eat and drink with him. After the meal he weighed a large amount of oil for him, as much as his money could buy. Then the rich man asked the messenger: "Do you have enough oil now, or do you want more?"

"I would gladly buy more, but I don't have any more money," answered the messenger.

"It doesn't matter. You will pay me another time," the rich man said. "I will go back with you to your native city and you will pay me whatever you owe me."

The messenger readily agreed and bought more oil. After that he hired all the horses and donkeys, all the oxen and camels in the Land of Israel, and loaded all the jugs of oil he had bought.

The messenger returned to his native Lodkia with the man who sold him the oil. When the people of Lodkia saw the long caravan approaching, they came forward to meet it with great joy. Happily they praised the messenger and said, "There is not another man as clever and as diligent as you, for you have succeeded in getting all this oil for us."

The messenger listened to their words and said, "Do not praise me, but praise this man who has come along with me. He is the one who is diligent

201 🌹

and clever. He is so rich that he alone had all the oil which I came to buy. Just the same, he does all the hard work in the orchard by himself. He appears to be poor, even though there aren't many men as rich as he."

When the people of Lodkia heard their messenger's comments, they accorded great respect to the owner of the olive orchard, because they realized that God blessed the labors of this hard-working man.

They paid him for the oil, and he returned to his home in riches and happiness.

Source: Talmud Bavli, Menachoth 85b

Food is not
for wasting

abylonia had a very fruitful year. The wheat came up and yielded a rich harvest. Flour was plentiful and bread was cheap. People became careless. They threw away the leftovers, and they wasted their bread. Food became a plaything to them.

One day, two people were standing in the marketplace and throwing bread at each other for sport and for fun. At that moment a wise man named Rabbi Yehuda passed by. When he saw the people playing around with bread and making a disgrace of it, he stopped in indignation.

"It appears that we have too much food," said Rabbi Yehudah. "People are so satiated that they have forgotten the commandment of the Lord: 'Do not destroy! Do not waste food!' If that is the case, then it would be well to have famine in the land, so that people will again remember God and His commandments."

Rabbi Yehudah was a righteous man, and God made his words come true. There was no rain that

year and nothing grew. No wheat or barley
appeared, nor were there any vegetables to be
found. The little food which was left over from the
year of plenty was scarce and expensive. People
waited in long lines to buy their bread. Some went
hungry and in their trouble they remembered with
sadness and regret how they had wasted their
food — when they had plenty! "We wish that we
now had just a little dry bread," they moaned.

Rabbi Yehudah did not know about the trouble
that had come to the world, for he was accustomed
to sitting at home all day and studying Torah, and
he rarely went outside. The other sages saw the
people suffering and said to Rav Kahana, Rabbi
Yehudah's helper, "You are always in the company of the righteous man Rabbi Yehudah.
Arrange for him to go to the marketplace so that he
can see how hungry the people are."

Rav Kahana agreed and asked Rabbi Yehudah
to come out with him. When they reached the
marketplace, they saw a great many people standing in line near the platform of the only merchant
in the entire marketplace.

Rabbi Yehudah was surprised. "What is this?
Why are so many people gathered here?" he asked
in wonder.

"This is the only merchant who has food to sell.
And all he has are meager leftovers and peels of
dates. It is worthless food, and yet the hunger is so

"We must pray for mercy"

great that everyone is anxious to buy some of it," the people said.

"The famine has indeed come to the world," said Rabbi Yehudah. "If that is so we must proclaim a fast day — a day of atonement. We must pray to God for mercy. We must ask God to give food to hungry people."

He then turned to his servant and said, "Please take off my shoes." (On the major fast days of Yom Kippur and Tisha b'Av, we do not wear shoes.)

The servant barely managed to take off one shoe, and already it began to rain. Even before Rabbi Yehudah started to pray, the rain fell. That is because God instantly fulfills the wishes of a righteous man for the good of mankind.

The following day, ships loaded with rice and wheat from a distant land arrived in Babylonia. The food was divided among all the hungry people.

The people ate and thanked God for His gracious kindness.

Source: Talmud Bavli, Ta'anith 24

Kindness to animals

Noach and his sons feed the animals

efore the Holy One, blessed be He, brought the flood upon the world, He ordered Noach to build an ark and to bring into it his wife and three sons — Shem, Cham and Yefeth — together with their wives. God also commanded him to take into the ark all the species of animals — all the different kinds of beasts, birds and insects on the earth.

Noach obeyed God's command. He prepared a special place for each animal. He built a wide, roomy cage for the elephants, a barn for the cows, and a stable for the goats and sheep. He made sturdy cages for the lions and wolves and other beasts of prey, so that they could not go out and hurt the cattle. He built nests for the birds, and small cages for the mice and lizards.

Noach also prepared food for all of the animals, and he stored it in the storehouses on the ark. For every animal, beast and bird, he prepared its favorite food — straw and hay for the camels; meadow grass for the cows; barley for the horses and mules; the branches of trees for the elephants; and seeds for the birds.

The real work began for Noach and his sons when the waters rose and the ark was finally afloat on the high flood waters. They had to take care of all the animals and to bring them their food. Each animal had to be fed at the proper time and with the appropriate food. The lions, the tigers and the wolves were in the habit of eating at night. The chickens and birds wanted their meals during the day. This one wanted to eat at one o'clock and that one at two o'clock, a third at three o'clock, and so on.

All day and all night Noach, Shem, Cham and Yefeth were busy caring for the menagerie without stopping. Many times they themselves did not get a chance to eat and to rest. For how could they leave the wretched, helpless animals hungry and thirsty in their cages?

Once it happened that Noach was late bringing the food to the lion. The lion was hungry and upset, and he let out a loud and terrible roar. Noach heard the noise and he was frightened. "Oh, I have not yet fed the lion tonight!" he exclaimed. He ran quickly and brought a chunk of meat to the angry beast. But the lion was in such a rage that he struck Noach with his huge paw and hurt his leg. From that time on, Noach limped and had difficulty walking.

210

Nevertheless, he continued to take care of the animals and to provide food for them. Even when Noach, Shem, Cham and Yefeth were very tired and hungry, they would neither eat nor drink nor sleep until they had fed the animals.

There was one animal in the ark whom Noach did not know how to feed. This was the chameleon, an animal that changes colors. The chameleon sat in his narrow cage and stared at Noach sadly, not knowing how to show him what food he liked to eat.

Noach felt very sorry for the chameleon. He offered him grass and seeds, meat and fruit of all kinds. But the chameleon remained in its place, motionless and hungry. Noach was afraid that the chameleon would die of hunger. But God helped the chameleon because He wanted all the animals on the ark to remain alive. One day Noach happened to be standing next to the cage of the chameleon, slicing a pomegranate which he was about to eat. (He didn't take the time to sit down at the table and to eat his meals in leisure.) The pomegranate was rotten in parts and wormy. A worm fell to the ground in front of the cage. The chameleon quickly stuck out his long tongue, caught the worm and ate it.

Noach was happy.

"Do you like to eat worms?" he asked gently. "From now on you will not lack for food!"

211 🌹

"From now on you will not lack for food!"

Noach and his sons feed the animals

From that day onward he saved all the wormy fruits and vegetables, and the chameleon never went hungry again.

Noach and his sons worked in this manner all year. Finally, the Holy One, blessed be He, had pity on them and ended the flood. Slowly the waters receded and the earth was dry again.

Noach was happy that the animals would now be able to go out and find their own food, and the animals were even more happy because they liked to be free and to get their own food from the hands of God and not from the hands of man.

Sources: Midrash Tanchuma on Noach
Talmud Bavli, Sanhedrin 108b

David
the loyal shepherd

hen David, King of Israel, was a lad, he took care of his father's sheep. Every day he took the goats and sheep to the wide open desert so that they would not go off to graze in fields that belonged to other people.

While herding the sheep, David observed that the strong healthy goats rushed into the fields. Pushing the small, weak ones to the side, they consumed all the new grass hungrily, leaving nothing but hard stubble for the little goats.

Seeing this, David thought to himself: "This is not right. The tender new grass ought to be left for the little goats, who don't have strong teeth yet. The big, strong goats can eat the coarse, hard grass."

He had an idea. He built fences and made a separate pen for the baby goats, another pen for the grown-ups and for the sturdy young goats. He placed each kind separately in its own pen.

Early one morning David opened the pen of the baby goats. They came out happily, pranced about in the pasture and with their little tongues licked the ends of the sweet soft grass until they were satisfied. Next he took out the elder goats from their pen and they ate the grass that was medium-hard, neither too coarse nor too thin. Last he opened the pen of the strong, sturdy young goats. They had the coarse stubble and heavy roots which they could chew with their husky teeth. And so they were all satisfied. No one pushed the other to get the food.

The Holy One, blessed be He, saw this and said, "The person who has the wisdom to take care of the sheep according to each one's need, may come and be the shepherd of My sheep — the people of Israel!"

Therefore, God chose David to be king over all of Israel!

Source: Shemoth Rabbah 2

The donkey that kept the commandments

Rabbi Chanina ben Dosa had a donkey who was raised in his barnyard and was accustomed to carry the righteous man on his back from place to place. One day the donkey was grazing in the field, munching on the sweet grass contentedly.

Suddenly robbers passed by the pasture. When they saw the big, strong donkey, they said to each other: "Let's steal this beast of burden. We can load the heavy sacks of stolen goods on his back!"

The villains all agreed to this wicked scheme. They tied a rope around the donkey's neck and pulled him along to their hiding place — inside a hidden courtyard. When they reached the place, they noticed that the donkey stood there miserably with his head lowered sadly.

"This donkey is probably hungry and thirsty," thought the robbers. They ran and brought barley, but the donkey refused to eat. They got some water, but the donkey would not drink. "Maybe he is spoiled and used to eating barley which is better and less coarse," said the robbers in desperation. They tried to give him better food — but the donkey would not have any of it!

For three days and three nights the poor donkey stood motionless in the courtyard. He didn't taste a single grain, because he did not want to eat from the barley of the thieves. It was surely stolen grain, and even the tithe (one-tenth portion for the priests and the poor) had not been separated from it.

"What shall we do with the donkey?" said one of the robbers. "He refuses to eat and he doesn't drink! He is no doubt sick and he will die before long. Let's take him out of here fast!"

Quickly the robbers removed the rope from the donkey's neck. They took him out of the courtyard and shouted, "Get out of here as fast as you can!"

The donkey was very weak and wobbly from lack of food, but he was so happy to be free that he started walking quickly. He walked and walked all night. In the morning he came to the yard of his master, Rabbi Chanina ben Dosa. It was very early, and the barnyard gate was closed because the people of the house were still asleep. So the donkey stood outside, cried and brayed in a mournful voice, as if to say, "Please open the gate for me fast! I am hungry and tired!"

The son of Rabbi Chanina ben Dosa heard the braying and said to his father, "It seems to me,

Father, that the voice of the donkey I hear resembles the voice of our donkey which was stolen!"

"You are right, my son," answered Rabbi Chanina ben Dosa. "It is indeed our donkey! Run, open the gate for him. For three days and three nights he has eaten nothing, and he hardly has any strength left."

The son of Rabbi Chanina ben Dosa ran, opened the gate and let the donkey into the barnyard. Oh, how miserable he looked! He was so thin and frail.

They brought a sack of barley and he ate. They brought a pail full of water and he drank.

The donkey was happy to be back in the household of the righteous Rabbi Chanina ben Dosa, and to work again for his beloved master.

Source: Avoth de Rabbi Nathan, chapter 8

The Lord has pity on His creatures

abbi Yehudah was a prince in Israel. He was a saintly and holy man, and the people loved him. Out of respect for him they called him "our holy rabbi" or simply "Rabbi" for short.

The Holy One, blessed be He, also loved the saintly rabbi. And yet, once when he failed to show kindness to an animal, God immediately made it clear to him that he did not do right.

It happened this way:

Every day Rabbi sat in the synagogue, teaching the Torah to the many students who came to him. One warm, beautiful day, Rabbi was sitting with his pupils outside, in front of the synagogue, teaching them Torah. He was thinking only about the words of the Torah, and he did not pay attention to what was going on outside on the street.

At that moment, some people passed by. They were coming from the village, pulling a little calf with them. The people were taking the calf to the butcher. They wanted the calf slaughtered for meat, because they were preparing for a big family gathering.

When they came close to the synagogue, the calf suddenly broke loose and fled. He ran for protection to Rabbi Yehudah and hid under his wide coat. From his hiding place, the frightened calf moaned and cried, "Moo, moo!" as if to say, "Please save me!"

But Rabbi did not show pity for him. He pulled the calf out from under the folds of his coat. "What can I do for you?" he said. "Go! You were created for this purpose!"

The Holy One, blessed be He, saw this and said, "It is not fitting for a man so wise and so righteous to behave in this way! Because he did not have pity on the calf, I will not show mercy to him. From now on he will have great pain."

That day Rabbi started to suffer severe tooth-aches, and he was in constant pain. No doctor was able to cure him, for such was God's wish.

Years passed. Then, one day, Rabbi Yehudah's housekeeper was cleaning the house and in one of the corners she found some newborn mice. The mice were so tiny that they could not have run away. The maid took a broom and wanted to sweep them outside.

Rabbi saw what the housekeeper was about to do and said, "Leave them alone! They, too, have a mother who will be sad if she does not find her

221

"God pities all the creatures which he has created"

little children. It is written in the Book of Psalms, 'And His mercies are over all His creatures.' God pities all the creatures which He has created, even if they are as small and as helpless as these mice!"

The Holy One, blessed be He, heard this and said,

"Here Rabbi Yehudah has shown pity to animals which men often chase and destroy. Now I will show kindness to him."

And God cured the rabbi. From that day onward, he had no more toothaches.

Sources: Talmud Bavli, Bava Metzia 85
Midrash Bereshith Rabbah 33